Weird War Two

Dedication
To Cat, Lucy and Hugh

Weird War Two

Intriguing Items and Surprising Stuff
from the Second World War

Peter Taylor

Published by IWM,
Lambeth Road, London SE1 6HZ
iwm.org.uk

ISBN 978-1-904897-43-9

A catalogue record for this book is
available from the British Library.

Printed and bound in Italy by
Printer Trento

Every effort has been made to contact
all copyright holders. The publishers
will be glad to make good in future
editions any error or omissions
brought to their attention.

10 9 8 7 6 5 4 3 2 1

Front cover image: Three air raid wardens
wearing a new type of gas mask during
a mock gas attack, 5th April 1941. (Getty
Images 3436600)

Back cover image: Venus, the mascot of the
destroyer HMS *Vansittart*, gives the bulldog
spirit a sassy spin in this photograph from
1941.© IWM(A 3998)

Design by Carole Ash and Philip Gilderdale
at Project 360.

Contents

Introduction

WEIRD WAR TWO is an eccentric encyclopedia of the Second World War, drawn from the vast collections of Imperial War Museums (IWM). Far from being a hefty history of the war, it salutes the strange but true, the wonderfully odd and the endearingly dotty. It has come from many happy hours spent wandering through the archives, stopping every so often to rifle through an interesting-looking drawer or peek in a forgotten corner.

If you want to know about flying jeeps and exploding chocolate bars, this is the book for you. If you're wondering why the military designed a bra for pigeons or a compass that you wore on your teeth, read on. Don't forget to check out the surprising contents of Winston Churchill's cigars and the recipe for 'English Monkey'.

You'll find bizarre inventions, from a gun that shoots round corners to a bomb made out of bats. There are real-life James Bond gadgets, too, including deadly pencils and super-strong itching powder. You'll learn how to play golf during an air raid and how to spot an enemy agent hiding in your village (crop circles are a dead giveaway). You'll marvel at parachuting dogs and undercover pigeons, not to mention warrior insects.

And, of course, you'll meet some strange and fascinating people: from a spymaster who lived with a baboon to a gourmet grass cook; from women who knitted with dog wool to a bishop who thought air raid sirens should go 'cock-a-doodle-do'.

This book doesn't promise to deepen your understanding of the Second World War or to make you a genius at pub quizzes. But it does hope to amuse and baffle you, and to provide a tiny testament to the creativity, inventiveness and, above all, silliness that can flourish even in the darkest times.

A Very Brief Summary of the Second World War

The war officially started on 1 September 1939 with Germany's invasion of Poland and ended in 1945 with Germany and then Japan's surrender. The conflict was fought across Europe, North Africa and Asia. It was the largest and most destructive in history.

The Main Allied Countries
Great Britain and its Empire, United States, The Soviet Union

The Main Axis Powers
Germany, Italy, Japan

Supreme Leaders

FROM MINIATURE POODLES
TO FLYING SHARKS

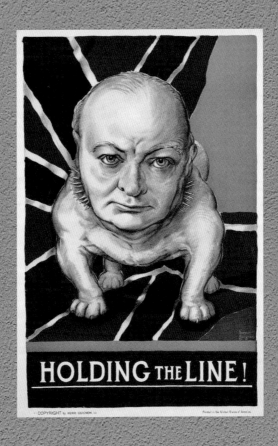

HOLDING the LINE!

PAGE 8
Winston Churchill holds a **tommy gun** in a morale-raising image from the dark days of 1940. Churchill offered to supply the king and queen with their own tommy gun in case of a kidnap attempt by German parachutists. The worried royals were already doing daily target practice at Buckingham Palace, while Winston preferred to perfect his aim using a rifle range under the House of Lords.

PAGE 9
He'll always be associated with **bulldogs**, but Churchill's own dog during the war years was actually a miniature poodle called Rufus. It could have been worse: an earlier pooch of his was named 'Pink Poo'. Churchill was a fanatical pet keeper — as well as dogs, he had cats, goats, pigs and a budgie. He even looked into keeping kangaroos.

WHAT DO THE SUPREME LEADERS of the Second World War, both Axis and Allied, have in common? All of them understood the cult of personality, for one thing. Leading your country during a war required a steadfast approach, with no room for human frailties. Emperor Hirohito of Japan was supposedly divine, so no problem there. Hitler pretended he didn't wear glasses, and Mussolini banned any mention of his birthdays to disprove the fact he was ageing. On the Allied side, Stalin chose a name meaning 'Man of Steel', President Roosevelt couldn't be seen in his wheelchair, and Churchill's heart attack towards the end of the war was hushed up.

They all cultivated distinctive gestures and trademarks, too. Hitler had his salute (read on for a very unlikely source ...). Mussolini's chin practically had its own fan club (of which he was president). Stalin was fond of the Napoleonic hand-tucked-in-coat pose. And of course there was Churchill's cigar and V for Victory sign. Churchill's dedication to his cigar wasn't just a public front — he even had his plane's oxygen mask adapted so he could smoke while wearing it.

If it were possible to put politics and morality aside, who would you want to have a drink with? Probably Churchill, provided you could keep up. Roosevelt would mix you a foul martini. Stalin would toast you into the ground. And the rest of them were more or less teetotal.

Follow the Führer Above the Clouds, one of a series of surreal **propaganda images** offered to the Ministry of Information by war artist Paul Nash. The Ministry thought they were unlikely to be understood by the public and turned them down. (Or perhaps they were trying to avoid starting a panic about flying Nazi sharks.)

A CRASH COURSE ON LEADING PERSONALITIES

Winston Churchill

Winston Churchill found fame and power as a soldier and politician at the height of the British Empire. He fell into 'the wilderness' in the 1930s, becoming out of step with the establishment in many ways, including his belief that Britain should arm against the threat of Nazi Germany. Vindicated by the outbreak of war, he became prime minister in 1940 at the age of 65. An inspirational leader, albeit a highly idiosyncratic and sometimes controversial one, he helped to keep resistance alive throughout occupied Europe and skilfully fostered the alliance with Roosevelt and Stalin that won the war.

Adolf Hitler

Adolf Hitler was the leader of the Nazi Party, an extreme right-wing group that took power in Germany in the early 1930s. His remilitarisation and aggressive expansion of Germany ultimately resulted in the outbreak of the Second World War in September 1939. By 1941 much of Europe was under German occupation. However, Hitler's decision to invade the Soviet Union and declare war on the United States in that year turned Germany's fortunes. Hit with defeat after defeat, Hitler committed suicide in Berlin in 1945 as Soviet forces entered the city.

Franklin D Roosevelt

Franklin D Roosevelt overcame debilitating polio to lead America through the troubled Depression era. Determined that his country should be the 'Arsenal of Democracy' in spite of its neutral status, he supplied Britain and China with weapons against the Axis powers until the Japanese attack on Pearl Harbor brought America into the war in 1941. Under Roosevelt America's military and industrial power transformed the Allies' fortunes. His health declined towards the end of the war and he died in 1945, succeeded by Harry S Truman.

Benito Mussolini

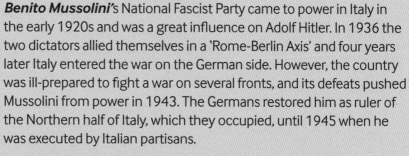

Benito Mussolini's National Fascist Party came to power in Italy in the early 1920s and was a great influence on Adolf Hitler. In 1936 the two dictators allied themselves in a 'Rome-Berlin Axis' and four years later Italy entered the war on the German side. However, the country was ill-prepared to fight a war on several fronts, and its defeats pushed Mussolini from power in 1943. The Germans restored him as ruler of the Northern half of Italy, which they occupied, until 1945 when he was executed by Italian partisans.

Josef Stalin

Josef Stalin became leader of the Soviet Union in 1924, purging enemies real and imagined and implementing radical agricultural and industrial policies at great human cost. As war threatened in 1939, he made the error of trusting fellow dictator Adolf Hitler to keep his word. Their non-aggression pact was shattered by the Nazi invasion of Russia in 1941. Stalin joined the Allies, but it was only in 1944 that British and American troops started fighting alongside the Russians in Europe. This delay only added to Stalin's suspicions of the West. Coupled with his territorial ambitions, it laid the ground for the Cold War from 1945.

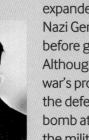

Emperor Hirohito

Emperor Hirohito was widely believed to be divine in pre-war Japan, but in reality his power was largely symbolic. Throughout the 1930s Japan was ruled by a series of nationalistic military leaders, who expanded their territory into China. In 1940 they made a pact with Nazi Germany and Fascist Italy. A year later Japan attacked Pearl Harbor before going on to occupy much of Southeast Asia and the Pacific. Although initially reluctant, Hirohito became a public supporter of the war's progress. However, setbacks made him critical and in 1945 when the defeat of Japan seemed imminent following the devastating atomic bomb attacks at Hiroshima and Nagasaki, he insisted on surrender when the military leaders wanted to continue. After the war he renounced his divine status and remained Emperor until his death in 1989.

WANTED

FOR INCITEMENT TO
MURDER

This gangster, who you see in his element in the picture, incites you by his example to participate in a form of warfare in which women, children and ordinary civilians shall take leading parts.

This absolutely criminal form of warfare which is forbidden by the

HAGUE CONVENTION

will be punished

according to military law

Save at least your families from the horrors of war!

The Germans loved Churchill's gangster look, too. They used the photo in this **propaganda leaflet** dropped over the UK. The text on the back begins: 'This gangster, who you see in his element in the picture, incites you by his example to participate in a form of warfare in which women, children and ordinary citizens shall take the leading parts.'

Same to you. Churchill's famous **V for Victory sign** started the wrong way round.

Apparently he didn't realise that using the front of his hand made it an offensive gesture. This picture is from December 1942. Churchill was already using the 'right' version by then, so perhaps he didn't like the photographer very much.

One of the less well-known passions of Churchill's life was **butterflies**. He stocked his gardens with them and planned to create a special house to breed them. His interest began as a prisoner of war in the Boer War in South Africa, where he used to pass the time watching butterflies in the exercise yard.

In 1941 Churchill was presented with 2,400 **cigars** by the president of Cuba. After Churchill handed some out to military and political bigwigs at a meeting in London, he cheerfully declared, 'It may well be that each of these contain a deadly poison.' They all lit up and lived to tell the tale, but nonetheless the cigars were tested. No toxins (other than the usual) were found, but there were traces of insect and mouse droppings ...

WEIRD WAR FACT

Churchill was a keen amateur bricklayer, occasionally brightening official visits during the war by seizing a trowel and laying down a line of bricks at nearby building sites. For a while he was even a member of the Bricklayers' Union, although his political views sat rather badly with them and 'Brother Churchill' was expelled.

It is believed that this **quilt** was made by the domestic staff at Chartwell (Churchill's home in Kent) from the freebie silk flags that came in Churchill's cigar boxes. Long periods spent sheltering during air raids provided the perfect opportunity to make the intricate bedspread.

The real Queen Wilhelmina of Holland.

In 1943 when Churchill sailed to Canada for a secret summit, there was an elaborate security operation to give the impression he was the Dutch royal. Signs in Dutch were added to the ship and Dutch soldiers drilled on the dock. Even his own daughter, who was accompanying him, didn't realise the deception until she reached the ship.

▶ Churchill invented the all-in-one **siren suit** to be quickly donned over his clothes if there was an air raid. He had ones for all occasions, ranging from military-style to flamboyant denim, pinstripe and even velvet. So, yes, the infamous 'onesie' is all his fault.

Churchill and baby Victor Lampson in their romper suits.

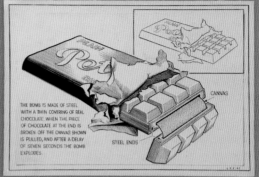

THE BOMB IS MADE OF STEEL WITH A THIN COVERING OF REAL CHOCOLATE. WHEN THE PIECE OF CHOCOLATE AT THE END IS BROKEN OFF THE CANVAS SHOWN IS PULLED, AND AFTER A DELAY OF SEVEN SECONDS THE BOMB EXPLODES.

CANVAS

STEEL ENDS

Death by chocolate. As part of their plans to defeat Britain, the Germans created **exploding chocolate bars**, which they aimed to smuggle into a dining room used by Winston Churchill and his war cabinet. Fortunately the plot was uncovered by British agents.

▲ Churchill's doctors advised it was dangerous for a man of his age and condition to fly above 8,000 feet. The answer: **a one-man pressure chamber**, complete with telephone, air conditioning, and – of course – ashtray. Disappointingly, Churchill never actually used the lifepod. They'd forgotten to check it would fit in his plane.

Ever the multitasker, Churchill didn't let his love of **long baths** interrupt his workflow, even holding meetings from the tub. When President Roosevelt visited Churchill's room during a stay at the White House, he discovered him pacing about naked after a bath, dictating. Churchill's deadpan response: 'You see, Mr President, I have nothing to hide from you.'

Stories abound about the eyewatering drinking habits of the three main Allied leaders, Churchill, Roosevelt and Stalin.

Each had a unique take on that classic gin and vermouth cocktail, the martini. Roosevelt went for mostly vermouth, adding a little gin and a few drops of absinthe to produce what most victims agreed was the worst martini they'd ever tasted. Churchill preferred neat gin, stating, 'I would like to observe the vermouth from across the room while I drink my martini.' Stalin probably preferred to observe the whole cocktail from another country, finding it 'cold on the stomach'. To be fair, his first martini was made by Roosevelt. Strangely, the main Axis leaders — Hitler, Mussolini and Prime Minister Tojo of Japan — were all virtually teetotal. What we can conclude from that is hard to say.

▶ A **Hitler toy** with giant moveable saluting arm. A psychological profile of Hitler, commissioned by America's wartime intelligence agency the Office of Strategic Services, attributed his arm-raised salute to an unlikely source: 'It is a direct copy of the technique used by American football cheerleaders.'

No photograph of **Hitler wearing glasses** was allowed, and he censored this one personally (after he'd put his specs on, no doubt). In another ruse to disguise Hitler's shortsightedness, his speeches and official documents were written with a special large-print typewriter with 12mm high characters.

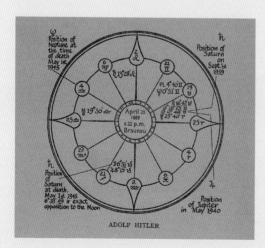

ADOLF HITLER

◀ Hitler's star chart. Despite all the rumours, Hitler was no great fan of **astrology**. But some people in Britain's secret services were certain he was being guided by the stars. How else could you explain some of his strange decisions? Astrologer Louis de Wohl was employed to second-guess his plans and in 1941 he undertook a propaganda tour in America, predicting doom for the Nazis.

▶ The author 'Pauline Kohler' was actually two British Intelligence officers. This lurid **1940 book** was written to tarnish Hitler's public image. The revelations from his real maid in 2008 were rather more mundane, including the fact that he liked to eat a special apple 'Führer Cake' before he went to bed.

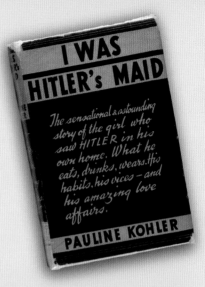

Equally **bizarre plots** planned against Hitler included lacing his vegetables with female hormones to make him less aggressive, and driving him mad by dropping pornography on his bunker (he was supposedly very prudish). Given that he was taking a vast number of drugs, from cocaine to extract of Bulgarian peasants' faeces (for his chronic flatulence), these plots seem almost redundant.

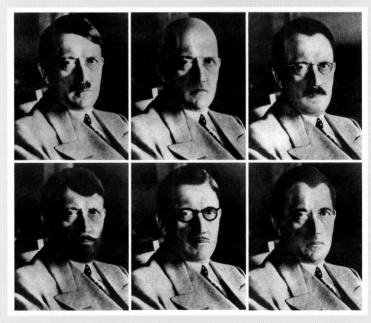

Towards the end of the war the Allies were worried that Hitler would flee Germany, so they asked a Hollywood makeover expert to suggest different ways in which the leader might **disguise** himself. Adolf doesn't look very happy with any of them.

A handy paperweight to remind you that **'Mussolini is always right'**. This slogan was the most famous of the Italian dictator's 'Ten Commandments'. George Orwell borrowed the phrase for the pig Napoleon in his novel *Animal Farm*, who was clearly modelled on Mussolini: 'Napoleon is always right.'

The **Italian people** probably didn't agree that Mussolini was always right, especially when he declared them a 'mediocre race of good-for-nothings only capable of singing and eating ice cream' and then banned the latter. His own favourite food was a raw garlic salad that further annoyed those around him.

Surprisingly, the Soviet leader Josef Stalin was a huge fan of American cowboy movies.

He used to criticise their capitalist ideology — then order another bunch. But when he drunkenly declared at the end of one screening that John Wayne — an outspoken anti-communist — was a threat to the cause, he set in train assassination plans. Fortunately they were cancelled by his successor.

Keep Calm

FROM PIPE GUNS TO
SUBVERSIVE JUMPERS

RIGHT ACROSS BRITAIN today you can still find the remains of secret Second World War bunkers. In 1940 you might have entered them by crawling through a badger set or lifting up a cucumber frame, or by rolling a marble down a pipe. It sounds silly, but it was deadly serious. The bunkers are all that is left of the Auxiliary Units – the secret guerrilla force that would attack the Germans once they had invaded Britain.

After Britain declared war on Germany in 1939, the first worry was that Germany would drop gas bombs. Instead, for eight months there was a period of relative quiet – the so-called 'Phoney War'. The country was gripped by spy paranoia. Agents were believed to be flooding into the country dressed as nuns, female hitchhikers and boy scouts. Just about anything was enough to arouse suspicion – from crop circles to 'idiosyncratic' clothing.

But then in May 1940 France fell to the Germans and suddenly invasion looked very possible. Britain ramped up its defences and created a volunteer army, the LDV (Local Defence Volunteers), later named the Home Guard. (There was also an unofficial Women's Home Defence Force, founded by Dr Edith Summerskill, who gained the memorable nickname 'Flossie Bang Bang'.)

Initially armed with little more than broomsticks and bravery, the Home Guard eventually became a well-trained force. Thankfully neither the Home Guard nor the Auxiliary Units were ever put to the test, partly due to the RAF denying the Luftwaffe air superiority during the Battle of Britain.

The legendary poster never saw the light of day, but even without being told to, Britons did their best to keep calm and carry on.

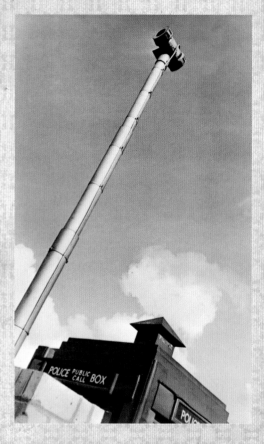

Children were understandably afraid of donning a gas mask, so 2 million of these colourful versions were produced and given the friendly nickname **'Mickey Mouse' masks**, even though the resemblance is a bit tenuous. For most children, the best thing about them was that if you blew] really hard you could make a loud farting noise.

These days **'Keep Calm'** seems irritatingly inescapable, but the original 1939 poster never saw the light of day. Over a million copies were printed and kept ready in case of invasion, but belatedly the government realised that its paternal slogan would annoy the public. They should have tried it on mugs and t-shirts instead.

As the Blitz took hold between September 1940 and May 1941, the sound of **air raid sirens** was an almost daily event. Many felt that the mournful rising and falling wail was dampening morale and tried to come up with cheerier alternatives. The bishop of Chelmsford's suggestion was a 'gay cock-a-doodle-do' repeated half a dozen times.

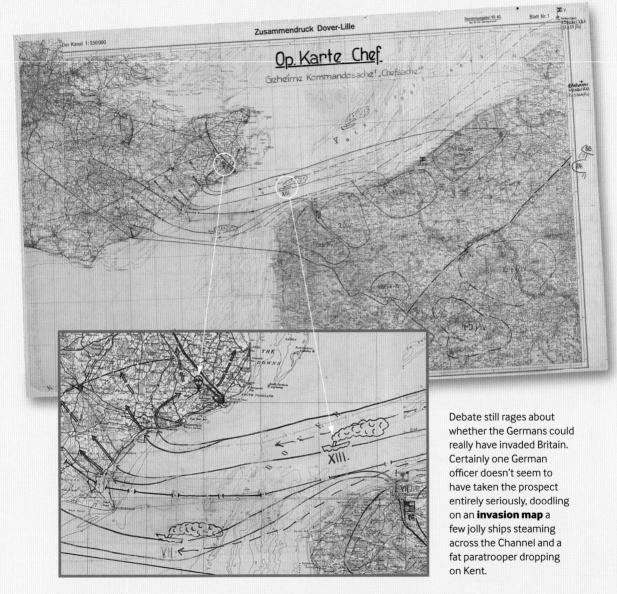

Op. Karte Chef

Geheime Kommandosache! "Chefsache"

Zusammendruck Dover-Lille

Der Kanal 1:250 000

Debate still rages about whether the Germans could really have invaded Britain. Certainly one German officer doesn't seem to have taken the prospect entirely seriously, doodling on an **invasion map** a few jolly ships steaming across the Channel and a fat paratrooper dropping on Kent.

On both sides of the Atlantic there was a panic that some farmers were creating **giant symbols** in their crops and soil to guide enemy planes to military targets. In the UK, MI5 investigated these 'signs'. They all proved to be coincidental, apart from one farmer who ploughed a hammer and sickle into his field to amuse his wife.

MI5 were also concerned about marks and graffiti on **telegraph poles**. Were fifth columnists leaving messages for each other? An agent was dispatched to look at every pole on the south coast, with instructions to ignore 'marks such as swastikas accompanied by scurrilous epithets put on by children or hobbledehoys'.

Next, a new threat was identified: **subversive jumpers**. A memo from a government official on 8 June 1940 noted: 'We have already discussed the possibility that Fifth Column personnel may wear some distinctive article of clothing – such as a yellow handkerchief or jumper. I think you have already circulated chief constables with a view to look out for such idiosyncrasies.'

A golfer carries on despite the unusual water hazards.

In 1940 there was a concern that **golf courses** would make perfect landing strips for enemy aircraft, so heavy junk like baths and water troughs was strewn across the fairways.

TEMPORARY RULES, 1940

RICHMOND GOLF CLUB

LONDON, ENGLAND

1 • Players are asked to collect the bomb and shrapnel splinters to save these causing damage to the mowing machines.

2 • In competitions, during gunfire or while bombs are falling, players may take shelter without penalty or ceasing play.

3 • The positions of known delayed action bombs are marked by red flags at a reasonable, but not guaranteed, safe distance therefrom.

4 • Shrapnel and/or bomb splinters on the Fairways, or in Bunkers, within a club's length of a ball, may be moved without penalty, and no penalty shall be incurred if a ball is thereby caused to move accidentally.

5 • A ball moved by enemy action may be replaced, or if lost, or destroyed, a ball may be dropped not nearer the hole without penalty.

6 • A ball lying in a crater may be lifted and dropped not nearer the hole, preserving the line to the hole, without penalty.

7 • A player whose stroke is affected by the simultaneous explosion of a bomb may play another ball. Penalty one stroke.

The very definition of stiff upper lip: these **Temporary Rules** were issued by Richmond golf club throughout the war after one of their buildings was hit by a bomb.

That's the spirit!

On the south-east coast of Britain four ladies carry on with their game of croquet while members of the **Home Guard** train to resist a German invasion. In the early days, the Home Guard was very poorly armed and probably would have been grateful for those croquet mallets.

THE GALE & POLDEN TRAINING SERIES

THE ART OF PROWLING
by
COL. G.A.WADE, M.C. Author of
The Defence of Bloodford Village 'etc

The delay in training the Home Guard led to a host of **unofficial military manuals**. Some of the advice sounds a tad odd now. One handbook not only warned to watch out for fake clergymen, nuns and farm labourers descending from the sky, but added 'adolescent enemy agents may be dropped in the uniforms of Boy Scouts or Sea Scouts'.

Well, 'Halt!' is easy at least. German lessons for Britain's last defence against invasion, **Local Defence Volunteers**, in 1940. When Churchill became prime minister, he gave the million-strong force a makeover, renaming them the Home Guard, despite objections that all the armbands would have to be reprinted.

A more high-tech concealed weapon: a **pipe that fires bullets**. It was invented by Mr V Marten-Gwilliam to give plain clothes members of the Home Guard a 'means of dealing with isolated enemy paratroopers in country districts'. The gun could even be smoked like a real pipe, although you'd have to be pretty brave.

Here they're making
Molotov Cocktail bombs.

Weapons were scarce in 1940, and arming the regular forces was the priority. So for the Home Guard, improvised and unusual weapons were the order of the day. The first stage of making the Molotov Cocktail was to prepare beer bottles by draining the contents. Hopefully there was a delay before stage two – filling them with petrol and tar, and adding a fuse.

LET HIM GO BY

THEN . . . . .

GIVE IT 'IM!

THE JOLLY OLD

MOLOTOF

▲ And that's pretty much all you need to know about using Molotov Cocktails. It's uncertain how effective this **weapon** would really have been against invading tanks. The same can be said of the 'sticky bomb', a sort of explosive toffee apple which was issued to the Home Guard after the army rejected it.

37

A special **armoured train** was built for the miniature seaside railway at Romney in Kent.

It looks more suitable for repelling a fleet of pedalos than anything, but the troops of the Somerset Light Infantry are giving it their best.

This **secret letterbox** hidden in a gatepost was used to communicate with an auxiliary unit in Devon. The Auxiliary Units were a highly trained, ultra-secret part of the Home Guard. If the German invasion was successful these small teams would conduct guerrilla warfare from underground dens.

By 1941 there were over 500 **hideouts** for the Auxiliary Units around the UK. Most were dug in thick woodland like this one, but some made use of natural features – in one case even a badger set. The trapdoors that led to the dens could be concealed by anything from tree roots to a vast block of chalk on wheels, or even a cucumber frame complete with cucumbers.

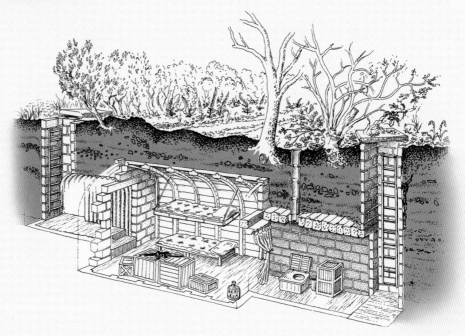

THE COUNTRYMAN'S
DIARY - - - 1939

HIGHWORTH'S FERTILISERS

DO THEIR STUFF UNSEEN
UNTIL YOU SEE.

RESULTS !

With the Compliments of
HIGHWORTH & CO.

YOU WILL FIND THE NAME HIGHWORTH
WHEREVER QUICK RESULTS
ARE REQUIRED

◀ This 1942 **training manual** for the Auxiliary Units was cunningly disguised as a boring, out-of-date diary presented by a fertilizer firm. The authors couldn't resist an in-joke though: like the units, the fertilizers 'do their stuff unseen until you see RESULTS!'

▶ Recruits for the **London Irish Rifles**, who fought the only invasion battle in mainland Britain. On 27 September 1940 soldiers from the regiment were billeted in The Sportsman pub in Graveney Marsh, Kent, when a German bomber crashed nearby. The crew miraculously survived and were overpowered by the London Irish, who bought them each a pint before they were taken prisoner.

Camouflage and Visual Deception

FROM PINK SPITFIRES TO INFLATABLE TANKS

PAGE 42
It looks like an audition for *Dr Who*. It's actually a group of soldiers demonstrating various styles of **camouflage clothing** in Somerset in 1941.

PAGE 43
Of course there's no point in camouflaging soldiers if you're going to give them bright shiny beer cans to drink from. The US government contracted 40 of the country's biggest breweries to produce special **olive drab cans** for their troops. Here's a can of 'Lucky Lager'.

AT THE BEGINNING of the First World War in 1914 camouflage had a pretty bad reputation. Many in the military thought hiding soldiers or artillery from the enemy was cowardly and underhand. In France *camoufler* was a slang term for criminals who skulked around the streets avoiding the police.

That attitude was long gone when war broke out again in 1939 (though a British Home Guard manual acknowledged some older members might still find the idea 'repulsive ... and not cricket'). It was the aeroplane that had changed everything. On the battlefield aerial reconnaissance could swiftly reveal the strength and position of the enemy. On the home front bombers could locate and destroy military and civilian targets. In the era of total war, camouflage had to be an integral part of attack and defence.

The military brought in a wide range of civilian camouflage experts. Zoologists, artists and movie people all played parts. Even a magician. Everything from beer cans to factories to entire armies was camouflaged in ever more cunning ways.

Visual deception was another clever way to fool the enemy, and often served to distract attention from what was really going on. The king of all visual deception campaigns was the D-Day invasion in Normandy, which included inflatable fake tanks and dummy paratroopers. That sort of thing might not be cricket, but it was very effective.

A **power station** is disguised as a village in this painting by Colin William Moss. Hiding Britain's factories and other industrial buildings from German bombers was the job of the Camouflage Directorate. This involved everything from painting and covering buildings to putting concrete cows on the roofs to make them look like fields. The unit received over 2,000 applications from artists, who faced lean times during the war.

The Americans took aerial camouflage to an incredible level, building entire **fake towns** on the roofs of the Boeing and Lockheed aircraft factories. The towns included mock buildings, trees and roads — complete with names such as 'Synthetic Street' and 'Burlap Boulevard'. Washing was even hung up and taken down in the back yards of the homes according to a strict timetable.

The world-famous botanical gardens at Kew in London were closed because of fears that glass or metal shards from the greenhouses might spear the public in the event of a bombing. But Kew was still able to help the war effort: here a curator oversees the harvesting of **chamomile** seeds. The plant was used as a quick-growing, wiry camouflage for new airfields.

In this painting by Edwin La Dell, a tractor sprays **dark paint** onto the telltale scarred ground around a factory to hide it from bombers. There was a similar scheme to camouflage the lakes and rivers that enemy planes used to navigate. Coal dust was spread onto the water from a ship (named HMS *Persil*, funnily enough).

A short-sighted tank driver might be fooled, perhaps.

As Britain prepared for invasion in 1940, thousands of small **concrete bunkers** ('pillboxes') were constructed to defend strategic points. Some of them were camouflaged — but usually a bit better than this one in Felixstowe.

Just down the road in Felixstowe, you could find a **concrete petrol station** for your concrete car. There was no fuel, but on the plus side it was fine to smoke, despite the warning sign.

Meanwhile, in Edinburgh there was a **concrete florist**. This may have confused some drunk husbands looking to buy a peace offering on their way back from the pub.

Sixteen tasteful shades from Craig & Rose, the leading supplier of 'battleship grey' and other **camouflage paints** to the Royal Navy. On the front line, camouflage experts sometimes had to take a more improvised approach. In the desert, there are tales of Worcestershire sauce and even camel dung being added to whitewash to create sand-coloured paint.

A.R.P. Camouflage Paints

Approved by Air Ministry for painting civil or industrial establishments, Factories, Warehouses, Aerodromes, etc. To give effective concealment and protection from aerial observation and attack.

The paints are available in two types, OIL-BOUND DISTEMPER and FLAT OIL PAINT, both are flat and non-glint and produced in gritty and non-gritty textures.

Oil-Bound Distemper type

Gritty and non-gritty textures, weather resisting, non-inflammable drying with a matt surface. Suitable for application to plaster, old and new cement, concrete, brick, tiles, wood and glass lights.

Not suitable for metal.

Covering capacity depending upon the condition and type of surface, approximately 500/600 square yards per cwt. or 50/60 square yards per gallon.

Flat Oil Paint type

GRITTY AND NON-GRITTY TEXTURES.

Suitable for iron and metal roofs, structural iron, vertical metal surfaces, also asbestos, plaster, old cement and concrete, brick, tiles, wood and glass lights.

Covering capacity, varies considerably, depending upon the condition and type of surface. Gritty 10/18, non-gritty 35/60 square yards per gallon.

NOTE.—New Galvanized Iron, not subjected to weathering for at least six months, requires treatment with Mordant Solution before being painted.

A.R.P. Black-out Composition

OIL-BOUND DISTEMPER TYPE.
Approx. covering capacity 500/600 sq. yards per cwt.
OIL LIQUID PAINT TYPE 60/80 square yards per gallon.

...erb Marking Paint

...capacity 60/80 square yards per gallon.

...e & Yellow Line Road Paint

...capacity 50/60 square yards per gallon.

M. & J. H.

CAMOUFLAGE PAINTS

No. 1   No. 5   No. 8   No. 11
No. 2   No. 6   No. 9   No. 13
No. 3   No. 7   No. 10
No. 4   No. 11a   No. 11b

TO OFFICIAL SPECIFICATION.
Shades No. 10 and 11 are always Non-Gritty.   Shade No. 14 is always Gritty.

CAMOUFLAGE PAINTS

CRAIG & ROSE Ltd.
CALEDONIAN OIL & COLOUR WORKS
EDINBURGH
47 BANKSIDE LONDON, S.E.1
85 CADOGAN ST. GLASGOW, C.2

◀ **Spitfires** used for photo reconnaissance missions during the day were usually painted blue, but those that went out at dusk or dawn were given a cute 'Camoutint Pink' colour to blend better with the sky.

▼ The snappy markings on these British **motor torpedo boats** may have been perfect for scaring German shipping. The thing is, the boats were also used to rescue airmen who had ditched in the sea. You can imagine they gave bleary-eyed flyers a nasty fright as they approached.

▲ HMS *Kenya* was nicknamed **The Pink Lady** because of her unusual camouflage. The British, American and German navies all experimented with painting ships pink to hide them at dawn and dusk. The British shade was 'Mountbatten Pink' (actually more of a mauve), named after Lord Mountbatten of the navy, who championed the idea.

There's something awfully British about these **giant ship umbrellas**, an experimental form of camouflage from the Royal Navy. It looks rather like the ship has stopped to take tea. The theory was that the umbrellas would help a ship to hide quickly next to land for defence or ambush.

▶ Confusing **dazzle camouflage** wasn't used as much in the Second World War as it had been in the First, but the US Navy in particular had a few amazing examples. This 'zebra' stripe design is on a torpedo boat (just the one, sailing towards you).

52

How many ships are there and which way are they sailing?

In this surreal painting by James Yunge-Bateman, a helper tweaks a model aircraft carrier in the **water tank** of the Camouflage Directorate. The tank was set up to test camouflage designs under different lighting conditions. Observers looked at the ships with naked eyes, binoculars and even mini periscopes to simulate the view of U-boat commanders.

One of the British Army's camouflage experts was a zoologist called Hugh Cott, author of *Adaptive Coloration in Animals*. In the book he identified nine kinds of camouflage used by animals in nature. The clever fish in this poster are using number four: **disruptive colouration**.

PERSONAL CONCEALMENT

EVEN FISHES HAVE GOT THE *idea!*

▲ Experts in camouflage and illusion recruited by the British Army also included the **stage magician** Jasper Maskelyne, seen here in a pre-war bill with Doris Cuban the dancing xylophonist. While he may have exaggerated his feats after the war — did he really make part of the Suez Canal disappear with mirrors? — he certainly played an important part in deception plots in the war in Africa.

Abracadabra! – a truck turns into a tank.

Jasper Maskelyne brought his magic touch to creating these **sunshield disguises for tanks**. It was part of Operation 'Bertram', a plan that successfully fooled the Germans about the location of an Allied attack in Eygpt. Some 500 dummy tanks were positioned 20 miles south of the real attack, while real tanks disguised as lorries trundled into place.

'Rupert' was a fake paratrooper

— a paradummy — used to sow confusion. He was about one third actual size, full of sand or straw and self-destructed when he hit the ground. About 500 were dropped to divert attention from the real paratrooper landings on D-Day. The dolls were accompanied by small teams of SAS troops, who played battle noises and launched distracting attacks.

Before and after.

Two soldiers carrying a deflated Sherman decoy tank, and the finished article. **Inflatable tanks** were used as part of Operation 'Fortitude', the plan to convince the Germans that the D-Day landings would be at Calais rather than Normandy. Legend has it that a bull once got loose in a field full of these tanks, with predictable consequences.

An officer inspects a German **dummy tank made of wood**, 31 July 1944. Wooden dummies were used by all sides for every kind of weapon and vehicle. The Germans built fake airfields on the Continent, complete with wooden planes. They obviously didn't do a great job, because on a couple of occasions it seems the Allies dropped wooden bombs on them, with messages such as 'Wood for Wood'.

This inflatable **'three-tonne truck'** actually weighed about 35 kg, a lot less than the soldier next to it.

▶ In 1944, MI5 sent an **actor** resembling one of the Allies' most senior officers, Field Marshal Montgomery, to tour the Mediterranean. The actor's job was to loudly discuss 'Plan 303', a pretend invasion in the South of France designed to distract the Germans from the real invasion in the north. It worked, even though M E Clifton James (seen here) was actually third choice to play the leader.

Soldiering On

FROM GREMLINS TO PANDAS

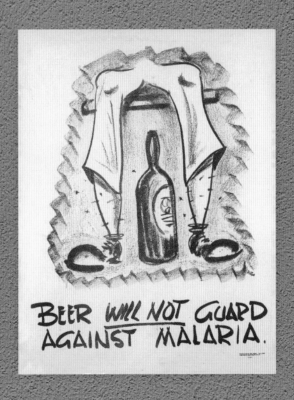

PAGE 60
Late pupils will not be tolerated. This photograph was taken at an **Infantry Battle School** 'somewhere in south-east England' in 1942. Battle schools were set up around the country to prepare new troops for combat. They taught physical fitness, tactics and a cool head under fire.

PAGE 61
But do cigarettes work? British troops fighting the Japanese were threatened by unfamiliar and deadly **tropical diseases**, including malaria. In 1943, for every soldier evacuated due to battle wounds, 120 soldiers were evacuated due to sickness. (A modern study showed that drinking beer actually makes you 15 per cent more attractive to malarial mosquitos.)

AS ALWAYS, men soldiered on, dealing with the terror — and boredom — of fighting a war as best they could.

Keeping fit was vital, of course. You had to guard your health. There were training films and lectures for that. And posters — lots of them — telling you to keep yourself clean and free of diseases, self-inflicted and otherwise. 'Beer Will Not Guard Against Malaria', one reads. Who knew?

You had to keep your chin up. Morale was everything. Even if things were going badly, you could find strength in your comrades. That shared sense of identity was fostered by many things, from pride in the glorious history of the regiment to special slang for grumbling about the daily routine. Sometimes it developed through membership of a club you'd hope never to join, such as one for surviving a plane crash.

For many, religion helped to keep the spirit strong. Mobile churches accompanied major campaigns. Every unit had its own chaplain, and the sheer number of nicknames he attracted shows he was a key figure in soldiers' lives: GI Jesus, Devil Beater, Sin Buster and Sky Scout, to name a few. Sometimes soldiers created their own mythology and supernatural figures, such as the omnipresent Kilroy and the mischievous gremlins.

One of the positives of being a soldier was the chance to see more of the world. Many had never left their native country and suddenly found themselves in strange new lands. Fortunately there were guidebooks to tell them how to have fun in Bombay, haggle in Venice and even cope with the boredom of an English Sunday.

◀ The Fleet Air Arm **gremlin** lurks above their bar. RAF airmen claimed these mischievous imps lived in their planes and caused unexplained accidents and mechanical problems. Author Roald Dahl had been in the RAF and his first children's novel spun a tale about these creatures and their wives ('Fifinellas') and children ('Widgets').

▲ It's fair to say there's some artistic licence here. This cartoon painting by Christian Maro shows the **squadron commanders** of the 145 Free French Wing of the RAF astride Spitfires attacking Germans.

It's not a style thing.

Night fighter and bomber crews

wore special **goggles** to accustom their eyes to the dark before a mission.

The RAF also ran special night vision training schools where gunners and bomb aimers learnt to improve their abilities with activities such as playing hockey while wearing dark specs.

A pilot tests the new K type one-man **dinghy** in the unlikely surroundings of Watford Public Baths.

This life raft was small enough to fit in a fighter plane and could conveniently attach to a parachute harness. It's unlikely any of that impressed the pool's lifeguard.

◄ British airmen who were saved by a life raft after ditching their plane in the sea could join the **Goldfish Club** and receive this badge. The extra wavy line here denotes a second ditching. The club was founded by the P B Cow and Company of Farnborough, manufacturers of rubber aircraft survival dinghies.

▼ The golden silkworm badge of the **Caterpillar Club**. The badge was presented by the Irvin Air Chute Company to airmen of any nation who had baled out successfully wearing one of their parachutes. At the start of war membership was 4,000; by the end there were 20,538 members.

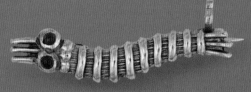

SEA SQUATTERS CLUB

This certifies that

"Turbo"

has qualified as a member of the Sea Squatters Club, having come down at sea and used a rubber life raft,

Jan. 12, 1945 in the Pacific

If a US airman spent more than 24 hours on a raft, he became a **Sea Squatter** and could claim a golden duck label pin and a certificate. The twist with the one shown here is that 'Turbo' was a dog, the mascot of a Navy Patrol Bomber crew, who had to ditch 500 miles off the Californian coast.

Formation badges were created as an easy way to identify military units.

They were worn on uniforms, painted on vehicles and used on road signs. The images chosen could be rather surprising.

◀ For example, the fearsome-sounding 1st Motor Machine Gun Brigade had a rather cute giant panda as their badge.

▲ The motto of No 1 Commando, meanwhile, was 'We hate lizards'. Only joking, the image actually refers to the myth that salamanders could come through fire untouched. (It was also thought that salamanders could make people's hair fall out by spitting on them, but that would have been less relevant and harder to illustrate.)

▶ The badge of the 2nd Anti-Aircraft Division, which covered parts of the north of England, pictured a witch on a broomstick. There may be a connection with the division's motto, 'We sweep the skies', or the 17th-century witch trials in Pendle, Lancashire. Either way, it's still a bit odd.

▶ The black cat was a popular symbol on badges, generally because of its association with good luck or because its nine lives matched the number of the division. The 9th Corps, formed to defend the north-east of England, had a 'Kilkenny Cat' — a term for anyone who is a tenacious fighter.

▼ This cat looks more worried than warlike. It's a shame, as this badge really needed to look fierce. The 17th Indian Infantry Division's original badge featured a streak of lightning, but after they were driven out of Burma and the Japanese radio propagandist Tokyo Rose called them 'the division whose sign is a yellow streak', they made the change.

◀ This cat is just plain cute. The 56th (London) Infantry Division's badge in the First World War was the sword of St George; for the Second they chose Dick Whittington's cat, appropriate for a London division. Ironically, in Italy the division was saved by a bird, GI Joe the pigeon (see the Animals chapter).

◀ This fat cat has swallowed a plane and looks like a spacehopper. This design was chosen by the 9th Anti-Aircraft Division in Wales, responsible for defending Cardiff and the South Wales ports.

It wasn't just civilians who were bombarded with **instructional posters**. There was no escape for soldiers either.

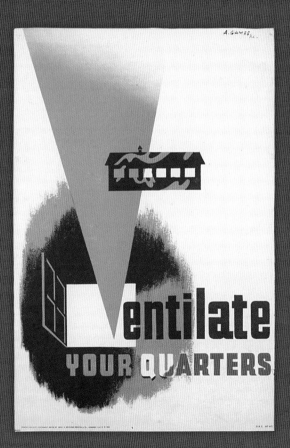

A.GAMES

entilate
YOUR QUARTERS

"**WHEN IN ROME...**"

DRINK AS THE ROMANS DRINK!

The ITALIAN knows the potency of the local WINES and treats them with respect.....
Remember that a LITRE of WINE contains nearly as much ALCOHOL as a PINT of WHISKY. A glass of vermouth may have greater effect on you than several beers, yet gives no warning of troubles to come.

SOME DRINKS CONTAIN:-
DANGEROUS POISON!
Drink only in
AUTHORISED BARS

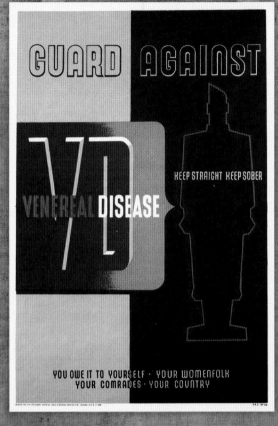

When the Free French pilots in the RAF went to liberate Europe they took with them this church made from the fuselage of a Douglas Dakota. Two official **mobile churches** were also built for the invasion of Normandy, with altars dedicated by the Archbishop of Canterbury to St Paul and St George.

For **Field Marshal Montgomery** the war was in some ways an extended caravan trip. This is one of three caravans that he used as his personal working and living quarters. It had two previous owners, the first being General Annibale 'Electric Whiskers' Bergonzoli, commander of the Italian 23rd Corps. This caravan became Monty's only home until the tail end of the North African Campaign in May 1943.

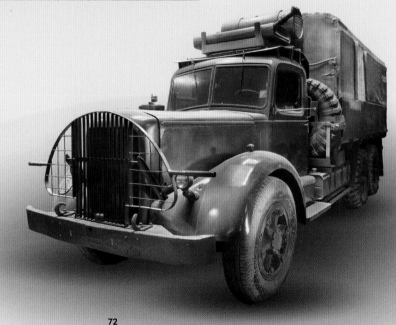

As troops travelled to foreign countries, official and unofficial **guides** were published about what to expect, what to do and what not to do. This one, issued free by the *Times of India*, is one of the livelier examples.

'The fireside of an Englishman', from **The English and Their Country**. The guide starts: 'The English have been called mad, hypocritical, impossible, ridiculous, cunning [and] simple', and pretty much ends up agreeing. In short, the English are as bizarrely variable as their weather. Only two things unite them: their love of privacy and their dedication to making Sunday miserable. Still, it could have been worse: a 1932 Dutch guide was titled *The English: Are They Human?*

The fireside of an Englishman

No one really knows where the phrase **'Kilroy was here'** came from, but it certainly tickled GIs, who daubed it everywhere they went. It even appears as a tribute on the World War II Memorial in Washington DC. The accompanying sketch of a long-nosed man was borrowed from another viral smash, Britain's 'Mr Chad', who appeared with the phrase 'Wot! No Sugar?' (or whatever else was rationed at the time).

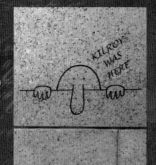

OPERATION ... TOENAILS

Every military operation had to have a codename. Here are some of the more unusual Allied ones. They don't always inspire confidence — Operation 'Crackers' and Operation 'Slapstick', for starters.

BABOON
BALDHEAD
CHATTANOOGA CHOO CHOO
CRACKERS
DRACULA
FRAGRANT
KAPUT
KNITTING
LENTIL
NOSTRIL
PIGSTICK
PURPLE WHALES
PUSSYFOOT
RASHNESS
SAUCY
SLAPSTICK
SUPER GYMNAST
TOENAILS
WEBFOOT
WILFRED

Some fine examples of US Army slang:

Army banjo — shovel

Bottled sunshine — beer

Bunk lizard — lazy soldier

Cornplaster commando — infantryman

Devil's piano — machine gun

GI Jesus — chaplain

Juice jerker — electrician

Khaki-whacky — woman excessively fond of men in uniform

Mickey Mouse movies — instructional films about personal hygiene

Misery pipe — bugle

Pep tire — doughnut

Retread — a First World War veteran fighting again

Sandpaper the anchor — unnecessary work

Uncle Sam's party — payday

After the defeat of the Germans in Italy, **Venice** became an attraction for thousands of Allied troops, who went there on leave. The gondoliers took this opportunity and upped their prices, forcing the military authorities to issue a list of official rates that sternly warned, 'Don't pay more! Be firm, these are the rates!'

75

Great Escapes

PAGE 76
A tunnel at **Colditz** POW camp. Colditz was a forbidding castle on a high hill in the north-west of Germany. The Germans considered it invulnerable and moved all the most determined escapers there from other POW camps. But after 300 escapes, of which a record 32 were home runs, they realised they may have made a crucial error: castles were built to keep people out, not in.

PAGE 77
'Moritz', one of two **dummies** who stood in for escaped prisoners during daily roll calls at Colditz. The Germans didn't cotton on until three months later, when one of the dummies failed to act on a guard's order. Another version of this ruse used 'ghost' officers, who faked escapes then hid and popped out to cover escapees at roll calls.

MORE THAN 300,000 Western Allied troops became prisoners of war (POWs) during the Second World War. POWs were always encouraged to escape, because even if an escapee didn't make it home ('a home run'), a manhunt would waste the enemy's time. European officers held by the Germans didn't have to work and were treated comparatively well. They had the best chance of escape. For Russians in Europe or any POW in the Far East, simply staying alive was the priority.

Some of the most famous escapes of the war involved tunnels. But there were many other ways of escaping – in boxes and bags, say. You could always just walk out of the front gate if you could pass yourself off as a guard or you looked convincing in a dress. Or how about flying out in a glider?

Of course, once you escaped your problems were far from over. Most camps had forgers and tailors who could help with the documents and civilian clothes required to make it home undetected, but the odds were still stacked against you.

British POWs, however, had two secret weapons: gadget geniuses Clayton ('Clutty') Hutton and Charles Frasier-Smith. They worked for MI9, the government department that equipped troops with escape and evasion gear and smuggled it into camps. Both were brilliantly original thinkers with a total disregard for red tape. They were also somewhat eccentric, particularly Clutty, who at one point hid his workshop under a cemetery because he was fed up with people borrowing his things. We've all been there.

Between them they produced miracles in miniature – tiny maps, compasses, hacksaws – that tell daring stories of escape and evasion that still amaze us today.

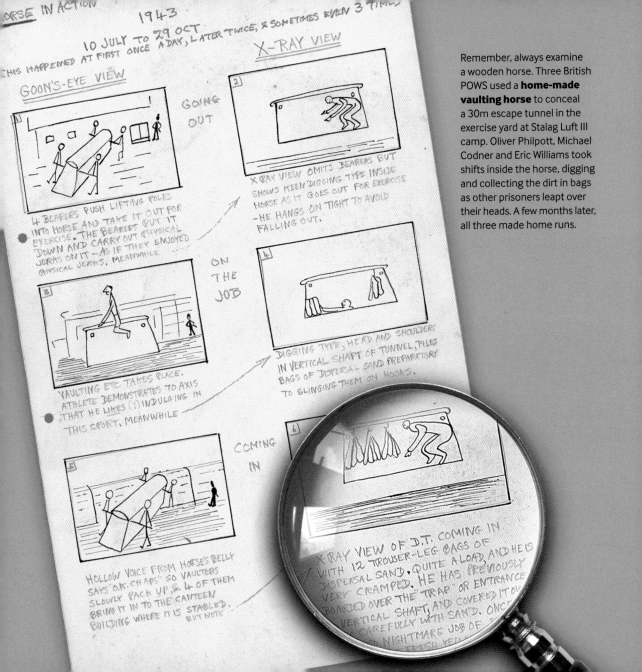

Remember, always examine a wooden horse. Three British POWS used a **home-made vaulting horse** to conceal a 30m escape tunnel in the exercise yard at Stalag Luft III camp. Oliver Philpott, Michael Codner and Eric Williams took shifts inside the horse, digging and collecting the dirt in bags as other prisoners leapt over their heads. A few months later, all three made home runs.

In 1942 Dutch POW C Linck tried to post himself out of Colditz in **a sack of parcels**. Unfortunately he was detected and returned to sender. Despite the best efforts of his fellow prisoners, his sack required two men to lift it, unlike all the others. Another snap for the Colditz guards' photo album.

Two officers successfully escaped through this hole beneath the stage of the Colditz camp theatre. A **trap door** was one of the nicer ways to exit the camp – unlike the sewers, which the British tried to escape through in the ill-fated 'Lavatory Break' of 1941.

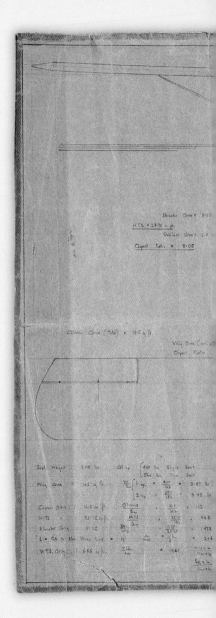

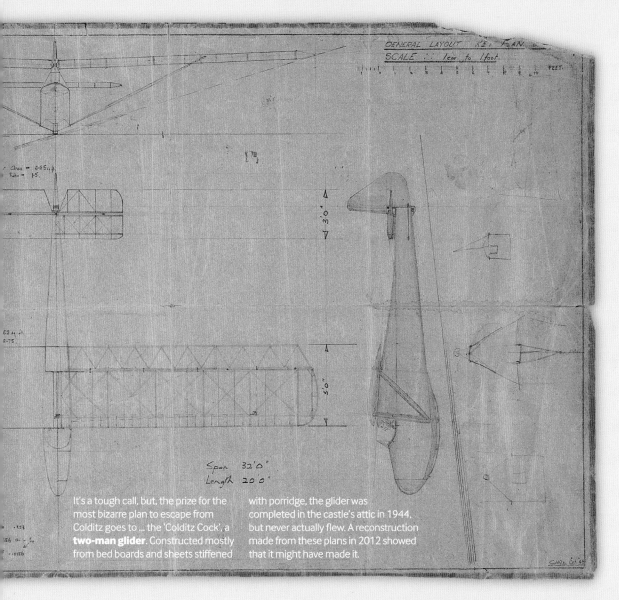

GENERAL LAYOUT KEY PLAN.
SCALE :: 1cm to 1 foot.

FEET.

Span 32'0"
Length 20'0"

It's a tough call, but, the prize for the most bizarre plan to escape from Colditz goes to ... the 'Colditz Cock', a **two-man glider**. Constructed mostly from bed boards and sheets stiffened with porridge, the glider was completed in the castle's attic in 1944, but never actually flew. A reconstruction made from these plans in 2012 showed that it might have made it.

WEIRD WAR FACT

Nearly 400,000 German POWs were held in camps in the United States. The Americans had their own version of Colditz – Camp Papago Park in Arizona. In 1944, 25 tunnelled their way out. They had hidden the earth by using it to build a volleyball court in the camp. They were all captured, although one – labelled the 'No. 1 Super-Nazi' by the camp's commander – lasted a month on the run.

One of Colditz's most famous inmates was RAF fighter ace **Douglas Bader**. He earned his place at the castle by repeatedly trying to escape from a camp in France. This was despite having two false legs, the result of a plane crash in 1931. Bader was forced to sit out the rest of the war in Colditz. Often literally, as the frustrated Germans took to confiscating his legs at night to prevent further breakouts.

These flying boots are made for walking. The **RAF 'escape' boots** were designed to quickly convert into inconspicuous civilian shoes for airmen on the run. The wearer just cut off the leggings with an enclosed knife. As a bonus the sheepskin leggings could be joined together to form a natty waistcoat.

▲ The 1944 **'Great Escape'** from Stalag Luft III in Germany was an incredibly sophisticated undertaking. This photograph shows the bellows that supplied the diggers with air and the little railway used to carry the soil. Three tunnels were dug, but only one was used. The materials stolen to make the tunnels included 90 whole double bunk beds, 3,424 towels and 478 spoons. Of the 76 Allied airmen who escaped, all but 3 were recaptured, and tragically 50 were executed.

▲ Would you trust this man? Mike Scott, painted here by a fellow prisoner, was considered to have a **suspicious face**. This was something of a problem when digging escape tunnels under the Germans' noses. As an acquaintance of his noted 'Mike always looked sinister... looking right and left with a sombre glare, so much that suspicions were aroused immediately even when he was doing nothing.'

◀ It was a **penguin**'s job to hide the sand and earth from the Great Escape tunnels. The bags you can see hanging at his sides would normally be inside his trouser legs. He would waddle up to a prisoner tending an allotment and pull a cord to quietly release the dirt onto the soil. There were around 200 penguins, and they made over 25,000 trips disposing of over 100 tonnes of soil.

With this kit, Major Woodley, the **camp forger** at Oflag IXA in Germany, produced the huge range of papers that a POW on the run would need.

He forged everything from basic identity cards to permits to cross frontiers, and even fake personal letters from a wife or girlfriend.

A little **phrasebook** for use by British and American airmen evading capture in enemy territory. Note the helpful label, 'Not to be produced in public'. That would be huge mistake of course, but escapees betrayed themselves in a hundred smaller ways. Even the wrong kind of walk. One escapee, Sergeant Stanley Munns, was told, 'You must stop walking like an Englishman and take small steps like a Frenchman.'

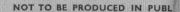

NOT TO BE PRODUCED IN PUBL

ENGLISH	FRENCH
I am (we are)	Je suis (nous sommes
British (American)	Anglais; (Américain)
Where am I?	Où est-ce que je suis
I am hungry; thirsty	J'ai faim. J'ai soif
Can you hide me?	Pouvez-vous me cach
I need civilian clothes	J'ai besoin de vêtem
How much do I owe you?	Combien vous dois-j
Are the enemy nearby?	L'ennemi est-il près
Where is the frontier?	Où est la frontière
BELGIAN	Belge
SWISS; SPANISH:	Suisse, Espagnole
Where are the nearest British (American) troops?	Où sont les forces (américaines) les ches?
Where can I cross this river?	Où est-ce-que je peu cette rivière?
Is this a safe way?	Est-ce que ce chem dangéreux?
Will you please get me a third class ticket to . . .	Voulez-vous me billet de troisi pour . . . s'il vo
Is this the train (bus) for . . ?	Est-ce-que c'est le bus) (car) pour
Do I change (i.e. trains)?	Dois-je changer d
At what time does the train (bus) leave for . . . ?	A quelle heure train (autobus)
Right; left; straight on	A droite; à gauch
Turn back; stop	Revenez en arri vous
Thank you; please	Merci; s'il vous p
Yes; No	Oui; Non
Good morning; afternoon	Bonjour
Good evening; Night	Bonsoir
Consulate	Consulat
Out of bounds; Forbidden	Défense de péné défendu

FRENCH
DUTCH
GERMAN
SPANISH

NOT
TO BE PRODUCED
IN PUBLIC

Twist this uniform button anticlockwise and – hey presto – a **tiny compass**.

Later on, compasses and other escape items unscrewed the other way. The theory was that it would never occur to the Germans to twist the 'wrong' way. Over 2 million concealed compasses were issued to British servicemen to assist with escape and evasion.

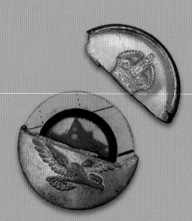

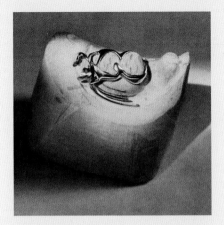

The hole in this **bar of soap** was made by a German guard at Colditz looking for concealed items.

Searches were a regular fact of life in all camps.

The Rolls-Royce of concealed compasses came with this gold made-to-measure holder that fitted over a **tooth**. The jaws on the left gripped the compass and the prong at the bottom held a tiny gold tube with a map or secret message inside.

To avoid being rumbled in searches, some British officers kept their maps and other escape gear in a **cigar tube** inserted where a cigar tube shouldn't go. Supposedly, the idea was inspired by the name of a particular cigar brand — Henry Upmann. The ploy was effective but uncomfortable. One POW noted, 'I would walk around like a cowboy.'

Lead the way. Part of the lead of this pencil is a strip of magnetised steel that works as a **compass** when hung on a bit of thread. To make these doctored pencils inconspicuous, well-chewed stumps were collected from schools in London. Pencils could also conceal flexible saws, called giglis, normally used by surgeons for sawing through skulls.

An **'escape' hairbrush** with a hollowed-out compartment that could hold a compass, a large map and a little double-edged saw. The joint around the lid was hidden with a coating of dandruff, which probably discouraged close inspection!

Escapist entertainment. The box for this game had a tissue map and compass hidden in its walls. Games, books and musical instruments were all popular ways of smuggling **escape aids** into camps. The parcels would be sent from fake charitable organisations created by MI9. A few normal parcels would be sent to allay suspicions before the 'naughty' ones started to go through.

The "Queen Mary" PUZZLE

INSTRUCTIONS

Escape maps were printed on silk as well as thin paper. So inevitably, not all were used for their rightful purpose ... This **bra and knickers** set was made up for Countess Mountbatten from a silk escape map given to her by her RAF boyfriend.

PRISONERS' LEISURE HOURS FUND

*" The treasures to be found in idle hours—
only those who seek may find."*

Runyon.

President :
B. ATTENBOROUGH, Esq.

Vice-Presidents :
Sir THOMAS BERNEY, Bart.
L. C. UNDERHILL, Esq.

Committee:
Lady D. BROWNE.
The Hon. Mrs. E. FREEMAN.
P. O. NORTON, Esq.
J. B. WORLES, Esq.

**66 BOLT COURT,
FLEET STREET,
LONDON, E.C.4.**

Hon. Treasurer :
E. TOWNSEND, Esq., C.A.

Hon. Secretary :
Miss FREDA MAPPIN.

Telephone :
CENTRAL 3951

12th MAY, 1941

Dear Sir,

Through the kindness of one of our
contributors, we are enabled to send to you a
selection of Musical Instruments - and Gramophone
Records, and we are having despatched direct from the
manufacturers in the course of a few days some records.

We intend despatching different selections
for each prisoner of war - to whom we send these, and
it is hoped in order that all may enjoy the variety,
you will offer to interchange with each other.

Further supplies will be sent you at regular
intervals, and if there is any particular record you
desire sent, perhaps you will look through the Catalogues
we are sending letting us know the make and number, and
we will do our best to despatch to you in due course.

Trusting you are enjoying good health, and
looking on the bright side of things.

Yours faithfully,

Secretary.

A Voluntary Fund formed for the purpose of sending Comforts, Games, Books, etc. to British Prisoners of War.

The covering note for a **naughty parcel** of musical instruments and gramophone records with hidden extras. As always, the letterhead contains clues for the POWs about the contents. There's the worthy quotation '... those who seek may find', and the organisation's address: 'Bolt Court'.

The hole in this **bar of soap** was made by a German guard at Colditz looking for concealed items.

Searches were a regular fact of life in all camps.

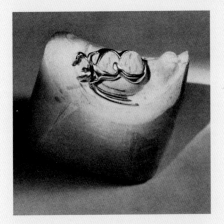

The Rolls-Royce of concealed compasses came with this gold made-to-measure holder that fitted over a **tooth**. The jaws on the left gripped the compass and the prong at the bottom held a tiny gold tube with a map or secret message inside.

To avoid being rumbled in searches, some British officers kept their maps and other escape gear in a **cigar tube** inserted where a cigar tube shouldn't go. Supposedly, the idea was inspired by the name of a particular cigar brand – Henry Upmann. The ploy was effective but uncomfortable. One POW noted, 'I would walk around like a cowboy.'

Lead the way. Part of the lead of this pencil is a strip of magnetised steel that works as a **compass** when hung on a bit of thread. To make these doctored pencils inconspicuous, well-chewed stumps were collected from schools in London. Pencils could also conceal flexible saws, called giglis, normally used by surgeons for sawing through skulls.

An **'escape' hairbrush** with a hollowed-out compartment that could hold a compass, a large map and a little double-edged saw. The joint around the lid was hidden with a coating of dandruff, which probably discouraged close inspection!

Escapist entertainment. The box for this game had a tissue map and compass hidden in its walls. Games, books and musical instruments were all popular ways of smuggling **escape aids** into camps. The parcels would be sent from fake charitable organisations created by MI9. A few normal parcels would be sent to allay suspicions before the 'naughty' ones started to go through.

The "Queen Mary" PUZZLE

INSTRUCTIONS

Escape maps were printed on silk as well as thin paper. So inevitably, not all were used for their rightful purpose ... This **bra and knickers** set was made up for Countess Mountbatten from a silk escape map given to her by her RAF boyfriend.

Keep Mum

FROM OLGA PULLOFFSKI TO THE
ANTI-LIES BUREAU

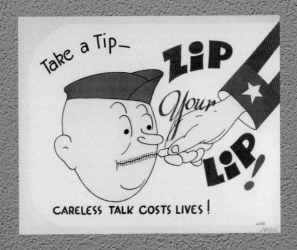

PAGE 90
Dad keeps Mum stuffed inside his shirt by the looks of it. An oddly-shaped reminder from 1940 that **'Careless Talk Costs Lives'**. The 'Be Like Dad – Keep Mum!' slogan was a great source of irritation to housewives, as Labour MP Dr Edith Summerskill pointed out to the minister of information in Parliament.

PAGE 91
In 1942 America's posters warned **jabbering servicemen** to 'Button Your Lip'. A year later, a more modern – and catchy – version appeared.

AT THE BEGINNING of the Second World War it was believed that German agents were lurking around every corner. So it was hardly surprising that the government was worried about people blabbing secrets — what their factory was making, for example, or when ships were sailing. The Ministry of Information issued posters, newspaper adverts and short films advising the public to keep quiet. It even managed to have the lights brightened in railway carriages at night to encourage people to read rather than chat with strangers. But by the middle of the war, the government had decided the real threat wasn't German agents eavesdropping on civilians, but rather glamorous females loosening the tongues of servicemen. Cue a memorably lurid series of posters and catchphrases warning hapless men of the risks.

There was also the problem of general 'careless talk', such as frightening rumours and defeatism. In summer 1940, when invasion seemed imminent, the government issued posters that called gossipers and grumblers fifth columnists, and there were some well-publicised prosecutions. This authoritarian approach sat badly with the British public. The Ministry of Information was forced to find a compromise, advising: 'Talk, grumble, but give nothing away.' Subsequent campaigns were lighter and more humorous, and there were attempts to disprove rather than simply ban rumours.

But the government wasn't above a bit of rumour-mongering itself, particularly when invasion loomed. According to fibs put out by a special committee, the English Channel was defended by some incredible new weapons with rather snappy jaws...

BE WISE

THERE ARE EYES

C.W. YOUNG, 1640,
TECHNICAL DEPT.
SWITCH HOUSE,
Nº 9 DOCK.

Some posters took an **abstract** angle to the threat of enemy eavesdroppers, with rather bizarre results. Another campaign at this time warned that 'The Enemy Has Long Ears'.

The Australians didn't pussyfoot about when it came to telling people to keep their mouths shut.

Here are four straight-talking **posters from Down Under**. If you don't know what BF stands for, let's just say it's not complimentary.

SECURITY SHAKE-UP No. 3

TYPES OF B.Fs

THE "SMART ALEC"

Thinks its pretty clever to dodge the censor, to work a code or post letters outside camp. Well, it doesn't get him anywhere, delays his mail and can easily bring death to his cobbers......Nice work!

POOR TYPE!

WRITE ABOUT YOURSELF—NOT THE ARMY

ISSUED BY H.Q. VIC. L OF C AREA

HOLD YOUR TONGUE

FOR OFFICIAL USE ONLY

Bad show! The British took a rather more polite and diffident approach to the same subject, at least to start with.

Bletchley Park was home to Britain's greatest military secret. It was there that the German military codes were being cracked, giving the Allies a war-winning advantage. As you'd expect, Bletchley took a particularly comprehensive approach to silencing its workers. A notice warned:

Sometimes people got in trouble for revealing secrets without even realising. In 1944 codenames related to D-Day kept appearing as solutions in the *Daily Telegraph* crossword. The setter, a headmaster called Leonard Dawes, was arrested by MI5, who suspected he was communicating with German agents. Eventually it turned out that one of his pupils was the culprit. Dawes would get his boys to suggest words for his crosswords, then he'd make up clues for them. The boy in question put in interesting-sounding words he'd heard from soldiers at a nearby military camp: Gold, Sword, Utah, Omaha, Overlord, Mulberry and Neptune.

Another person who may not have realised that she was revealing a secret was the **medium Helen Duncan**. Her séances tended to have a 'Blue Peter' touch — she made spirits from magazine photographs and ectoplasm from cheesecloth. But during one of them she somehow hit upon the fact that HMS *Barham* had been sunk. The authorities were keeping this strictly secret to preserve morale, and Duncan was convicted under the Witchcraft Act of 1735 and jailed for nine months.

By the middle of the war the government seemed to decide the biggest danger was **beautiful female spies** pumping boastful servicemen for information. The public nicknamed the glamorous blonde who appeared in all these posters 'Olga' after the 1930s comic song, 'Olga Pulloffski, the Beautiful Spy'.

Tell NOBODY –
not even HER

CARELESS TALK COSTS LIVES

▶ Olga also makes an appearance on screen, in *Horace*, a **cautionary melodrama** for servicemen. She flatters the diminutive RAF hero into proposing. He takes her to meet his parents, who are suspicious — and rightly so, as she soon tries to goad him into revealing secrets. In the nick of time, the authorities turn up to arrest her: 'Don't muck about, hold your horses, this is Olga the beautiful spy and her job is getting dope from the Forces!'

You forget – but she REMEMBERS

CARELESS TALK COSTS LIVES

PAY NO HEED TO RUMOURS

OFFICIAL NEWS WILL BE ISSUED FREELY!

As well as clamping down on people leaking information, the government tried to stop them **listening to rumours**, which it worried could create confusion and damage morale.

WEIRD WAR FACT

In Boston, an experimental **Rumor Clinic** was set up. A network of 300 'morale wardens' tracked down 'wild, damaging, morale-eroding stories' and the local newspaper printed corrections. So, for example, they were able to disprove the tale of the female ammunition worker whose head exploded when she went for a perm. A similar scheme, the Anti-Lies Bureau, was started by Britain's Ministry of Information.

▼ Of course, the right kind of rumour could prove helpful. The British government primed people to spread false rumours wherever they thought German spies were active. They even recruited aristocrats and socialites to spread misinformation at **cocktail parties**, although some were a little too indiscrete to be believable. As one government official said of the peer Lady Willingdon, she was 'a little apt to tell everyone everything she knows on all possible occasions'.

▲ The Underground Propaganda Committee was the source of Britain's sneakiest rumours, particularly those exaggerating its military strength as the German invasion loomed in 1940. The strangest of these fabrications was that the Australian government had supplied 200 **sharks** to roam the English Channel and eat any Germans who fell in.

Weapons and Inventions

FROM FLYING JEEPS
TO BAT BOMBS

PAGE 102
It'll never fly! This bizarre helicopter-like device is actually a **Goertz Sound Locator**. Before radar was invented later in the war, these giant ear trumpets were the state-of-the-art equipment for tracking enemy aircraft.

PAGE 103
The US military investigated the possibility of **pigeon-guided bombs**. The birds were trained by famous psychologist B F Skinner to sit inside bombs and steer them by pecking at the target on a screen. Unsurprisingly, the experience unnerved the pigeons, so they were fed hemp before the mission. The project was cancelled: perhaps the military didn't want stoned pigeons in charge of bombs.

THE SECOND WORLD WAR gave perhaps the greatest incentive to develop new inventions, both defensive and deadly, there has ever been.

At one end of the spectrum there were triumphs of high technology such as radar, which enabled the RAF to track German bombers on their nightly raids from up to 200 miles away. (Perhaps equally brilliant was the myth spread to disguise this invention – that our airmen could see in the dark simply by munching armfuls of vitamin-rich carrots.) At the other end, there were triumphs of improvisation and bravery. A mine that relied on an aniseed ball for its fuse, for example. Spider webs used to make precision instruments. Torpedoes that were guided by intrepid frogmen sitting on top.

Many inventions solved very specific problems. There really was a need for a swimming tank and a gun that could shoot round corners. Even a cute miniature motorbike had a point. And then there were heroic failures. To be fair, it was a time when almost no idea was too bizarre to be ignored – and often given huge stacks of cash to develop. Giant iceberg ships? Fair enough. Bat bombs? Worth a go. Flying jeeps? OK, as long as the seatbelts work ...

The legacy of inventions from the Second World War has shaped our lives today for better and worse. What is the most significant? The atom bomb? The jet engine? How about gaffa tape – the product that literally holds our world together.

A real life Chitty-Chitty-Bang-Bang **flying car**.

The Hafner Rotabuggy was an experiment in making a
vehicle that could be towed behind a bomber and dropped
off wherever it was needed. In the end, this jeep with a
rotorblade was replaced by vehicle-carrying gliders.

Yes, it's a **rifle that shoots round corners**. The Germans developed this attachment for rifles so tank crews could deal with attackers alongside them. There's a periscope on top so they could see where they were firing. A later version deflected the bullet through 90 degrees, but unsurprisingly it wasn't very successful.

▲ **Spider silk** was sometimes used to make the crosshairs for bomb and gun sights as it was finer and more resilient than wire. In Britain the Garden Cross was the preferred species, collected in matchboxes from moors near to the factories. In America there were private 'spider ranches' where deadly Black Widows produced silk for $20 per 100 feet.

◄ This canister was to house **a thousand bats**, each carrying a little napalm bomb. Released over Japan, the bats would seek roosting spots, setting the country ablaze. Remarkably, the inventor was able to secure a memo from the president stating 'This man is not a nut'. Wrong: the only blaze the bats started was at a US Air Force base when they were released by mistake.

▶ The limpet mine was a magnetic bomb that could be stuck to the side of a ship by a diver. Despite coming from the secret weapons research lab known as 'Churchill's Toyshop', it was a rather homespun affair. The inspiration was a washing-up bowl from Woolworths and the delayed action fuse was simply an **aniseed ball**, kept dry before use in a condom.

◀ Radar, the British invention that used radio waves to detect enemy aircraft, owes its creation to a pre-war competition to develop a '**death ray**' to incinerate enemy aircraft. The government offered £1,000 to anyone who could kill a sheep from 100 yards with a ray. Fortunately for the sheep, no one was able to do it, which prompted further investigations and the real breakthrough.

▶ This American woman sports a rather fetching Christmas knit whilst modelling the latest civilian defence gadget of 1942. The **portable sound detector** unit was designed to listen out for enemy planes approaching.

Space Mirror by James Lewicki © Estate of James Lewicki

▲ Speaking of death rays, behold the **Space Mirror**, without a doubt the most outlandish of the German weapon concepts. This vast mirror in space would reflect the sun's rays to fry a city or boil part of an ocean. In this artist's impression from *LIFE* magazine in 1945, the Nazis have selected Pittsburgh. A bad choice: it could be a while before anyone notices that its gone.

Churchill admires **'Nellie'**, a mechanised excavating machine designed to dig its way towards the enemy in a 5ft deep trench. It was very much Churchill's baby (a 130 tonne, 77 ft long baby), and it took him a long time to admit that it was a pretty useless throwback to the tactics of the previous war.

Airfields dogged by fog? Turn to **FIDO**, the British wonder invention. FIDO stood for 'Fog, Intensive Dispersal Of' and comprised a series of giant Bunsen burners that surrounded airfields and burnt the fog away to allow planes to land safely. FIDO was pretty thirsty, drinking up to 100,000 gallons of petrol an hour.

Giant sea fortresses were positioned off
Britain's coast and estuaries to protect them
from enemy ships and planes.

Up to 265 troops manned the forts in six-week shifts. Claustrophobia
was a problem, particularly for the crews sleeping below the sea in
the legs of the forts, and led to a condition called 'fort madness'.

If you're proposing to make an indestructible 2,000ft **aircraft carrier** from ice mixed with sawdust ('pykrete'), you need to be convincing.

Fortunately, Lord Mountbatten was up to the task. To demonstrate pykrete's incredible strength to the Allied chiefs of staff he shot at a block with a pistol, nearly taking out an admiral with the ricochet. To prove that pykrete wouldn't melt, he dropped a chunk into Churchill's bath while the PM was having a soak. Sadly, although preliminary tests were carried out, the ambitious Project Habakkuk was abandoned and the 'iceberg ship' never built.

Perhaps the smallest vehicle made in the war, the welbike was a **miniature motorcycle** for parachute troops or secret agents. It could be unpacked and ready to go in 15 seconds. The top speed was 30 mph — which would have been quite an experience, given that it had tiny wheels, no suspension and only one brake.

▲ It seems unlikely, but a canvas screen was enough to make a 30 tonne tank float. Powered by a propeller in the water, hundreds of **amphibious Sherman DD tanks** were used on the beaches on D-Day. The Germans went one step better with their plans for invading Britain, with the Tauchpanzer or deep-wading tank, which had a snorkel and could drive along the sea bed up to 15 metres deep.

▲ A Churchill **'Bobbin' tank** lays a track across a soft beach. Like the amphibious tank, this was one of 'Hobart's funnies', a collection of modified tanks and armoured vehicles specially designed to assist the D-Day invasion in Normandy in June 1944. The funnies also included the 'ARK', a tank that doubled as a bridge, and the 'Crab', fitted with flailing chains to clear mines.

▶ The most ordinary looking but most secret of all the funnies was codenamed the **'Canal Defence Light'**, a giant searchlight mounted in a tank. Its purpose was to light night-time operations and to dazzle enemy forces by flickering several times a second in different colours.

◀ The Focke-Achgelis Fa 330 Bachstelze ('Wagtail') was a tiny **gyrocopter** towed behind a U-boat. Rising to about 300ft in the air, a lookout could see much further than from the deck of a submarine. Luckily there was a lever to release the cable if the sub had to crash dive ...

▼ An Italian **human torpedo**, nicknamed Maiale ('the pig') for its dreadful handling. This two-man device was ferried near to the target by a 'mother' submarine. Once the detachable warhead was clamped to the side of the ship, the crew returned. Impressed by the Italian success against two of their battleships, the British copied the torpedo to create the 'Chariot'.

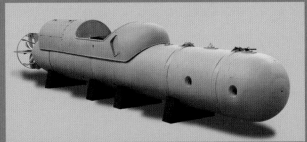

▶ A **Motorised Submersible Canoe** (MSC), also known as a 'Sleeping Beauty'. This mini submarine was developed to convoy frogmen for sabotage and reconnaissance operations by Britain's Special Operations Executive (SOE). As the canoe approached the target, the diver would sink below the waves, 'porpoising' up to the surface periodically to check his bearings.

The Department of Miscellaneous Weapons Development presents the **Great Panjandrum.**

This giant Catherine Wheel was designed to destroy beach defences ahead of the Allied invasion of France. Instead, it nearly destroyed a group of admirals during one of its test displays, forcing them to dive for cover as it rocketed out of control. Back to the drawing board.

One of the vast floating spools for PLUTO (Pipeline Under the Ocean), an **undersea petrol pipeline** to France. Without fuel, the Allied invasion of France would soon grind to a halt, but tankers were vulnerable to attack. By March 1945, the pipes were delivering a million gallons of fuel a day. The pumping stations were disguised as anything from beach bungalows to ice-cream factories.

Duct tape (aka Duck or gaffa tape) was invented in America 1943 to keep moisture out of ammunition boxes.

Troops loved it then as much as today's DIY-ers and gave it the nickname '100 mph tape' because it could even hold a speeding jeep together.

The war also gave birth to two less practical but equally beloved inventions — Silly Putty (a failed rubber substitute) and **Slinky** (from springs used to stabilise instruments on ships).

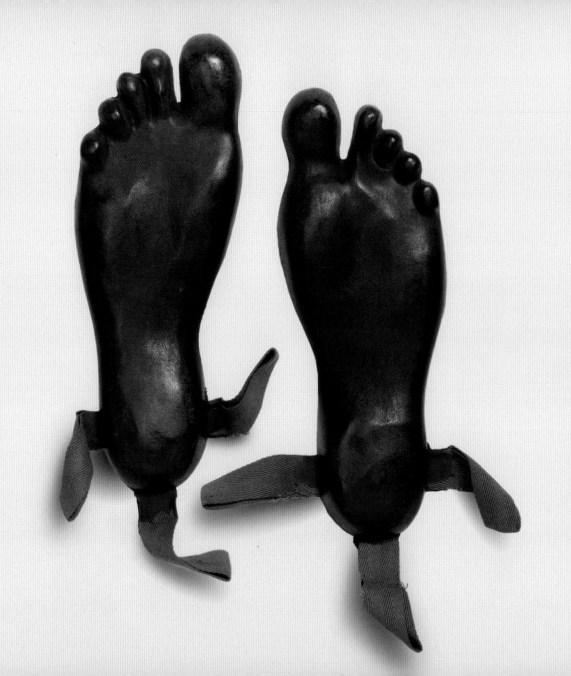

Secret Agents

FROM GARLIC CHOCOLATE
TO EXPLODING RATS

PAGE 116
The ultimate sneakers. These **overshoes** were made for Britain's Special Operations Executive (SOE) agents operating in South East Asia and the Pacific. When the agent landed on a beach from the sea, the 'footprints' were intended to fool the Japanese into thinking that he was a native.

PAGE 117
A **toy disguise kit** owned by Angus Fyffe, who worked for SOE in various roles during the war. Hopefully it wasn't used for real. One of Fyffe's jobs was at 'The Cooler' in Scotland, where agents who didn't make the grade were secretly sidelined and kept happy with pretend training courses for non-existent missions. Perhaps this kit was used in a fake disguise course.

DESPITE THE SPY SCARE early in the war, only 138 German agents were ever sent to Britain. Some were bizarrely ill-prepared, such as the pair caught cycling on the wrong side of the road and carrying German sausages. Many were poorly motivated and simply handed themselves in. About a third were turned into double agents and used to feed misinformation back to the Germans.

Meanwhile, Britain's own spy service, MI6, was busy operating networks of agents in Belgium, France and Norway. Despite the growing importance of code-breaking, aerial reconnaissance and double agents, there was still a role for spies on the ground – whether monitoring troop movements, coastal defences or the development of secret weapons.

In July 1940 a new volunteer force was created, the Special Operations Executive (SOE), whose job was sabotage and subversion behind enemy lines. The head of MI6, Sir Stewart Menzies, didn't take kindly to the 'amateur, dangerous and bogus' newcomers, but SOE was championed by Churchill, who wanted it to 'set Europe ablaze!' Its agents later also operated in the Far East.

SOE agents were assisted by an extraordinary array of disguises, gadgets and weapons, some of which inspired Ian Fleming when he wrote the James Bond novels. They included everything from lethal pencils to exploding camel droppings, all created by a team based in 'Churchill's Toyshop', a country house outside London.

Quite how effective many of these items were is debatable, but if they helped the confidence of the agents, that was something. Because being a secret agent often required exceptional confidence and remarkable bravery.

No. 1.

No. 2.

Make-up techniques used by SOE for overseas agents. The first two are temporary disguises; the second two show the same chap with 'semi-permanent' disguises. Occasionally 'permanent make-up' (i.e. plastic surgery) was used on agents with distinctive features who were well-known in their home country.

No. 3.

No. 4.

As well as being an ace spycatcher, the wartime head of MI5, **Major Charles Henry Maxwell Knight**, was a passionate naturalist who shared his flat with a baboon, a bear cub, lizards, snakes, birds, rats and tarantulas. And he liked to take his hobby to work with him. 'He always had something live in his pocket,' noted his colleague John Bingham. Knight is believed to be the model for 'M' in the James Bond novels (sadly minus the baboons and tarantulas).

WEIRD WAR FACT

A suspect but entertaining story of spycatching was told by American TV legend Lucille Ball. Apparently she was driving home from the studio when she heard a tapping sound in her mouth like Morse code. She told the studio's security people, who informed the FBI. The FBI investigated and discovered that the lead fillings in Lucille's teeth were picking up secret radio transmissions from a Japanese spy.

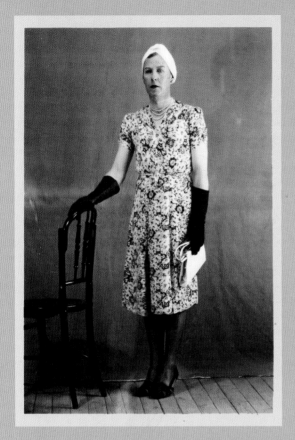

You had one job...

Lieutenant Colonel Dudley Clarke,
top British spy, was supposed to deliver
important papers to Egypt in October 1941.

Instead he got himself
arrested in Madrid for
cross dressing, as this
highly unusual mugshot
shows. At first he claimed
to be a novelist who
wanted 'to study the
reactions of men to
women in the streets'.
Then he insisted it was
all a prank. 'This hardly
squares with the fact that
the garments and shoes
fitted him,' the British
embassy noted tartly
before rescuing him.

Fake matchbox labels made for SOE agents in occupied France. Matchboxes could be supplied with fake bottoms for concealing documents. The smallest detail had to be right for agents to blend in — the right matchbox, the right kind of cigarette, the right lighter.

This **tiny camera** was developed by Kodak for use by America's secret service, the Office of Strategic Services (OSS). It was made in the shape of a matchbox and could be camouflaged by adding a matchbox label appropriate for the country in which it was to be used.

Reely clever: a **fake cotton reel** for British agents to hide films and documents. Other such gadgets included wallets with special pockets, hairbrushes and shaving brushes with hidden compartments, and shoe heels with sliding panels.

This **pencil** was almost as mighty as a sword thanks to the SOE workshop. It had a blade hidden inside, which could be removed by pulling on the twine wrapped around it. The twine was then used to lash the blade to the pencil to make a dagger.

SOE bought up a number of these American **gas pens**, which fired tear gas (and bullets with a few modifications). Later, they developed their own pen that fired gramophone needles. The idea was that French civilians could use them to harass German soldiers — particularly once they spread the rumour that the needles were poisoned.

A **tyre slasher** belonging to Agent Seahorse, aka Wing Commander Forest Frederick Edward Yeo-Thomas, who operated in occupied France. With the blade folded in, this sabotage device might just about pass for a coin. Yeo-Thomas was one of SOE's most famous agents, known to the Germans as the 'White Rabbit'.

▼ The room in the **Natural History Museum** in London where SOE demonstrated their gadgets to Allied dignitaries and VIPs. They also produced a mail order catalogue of their 'special devices and supplies' for their regional headquarters worldwide. It was nicknamed the 'shopping list'.

▶ Available from the 'shopping list': SOE's legendary **dead rat stuffed with explosives**. The rats were collected by a man in Tottenham, North London, who was told they were needed for scientific research. The rat was to be left on the coal near an enemy's boiler, where it would get chucked on the fire and the explosives would ignite. In fact, the first batch of rats was intercepted by the Germans. The resulting panicked search for other rats was far more disruptive than Plan A.

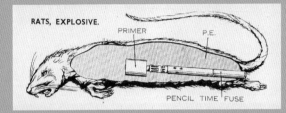

RATS, EXPLOSIVE.
PRIMER
P.E.
PENCIL TIME FUSE

The 'S capsule' was SOE's **stink bomb** on steroids. It could be chucked at enemy agents or dignitaries to embarrass them, or even used to put off dogs pursuing agents. The Americans devised a similarly whiffy weapon for the French Resistance, a spray amusingly called 'Who, Me?' It had to be scrapped because the person releasing the spray generally ended up smelling as bad as the intended victim.

One of SOE's boffins was concerned that agents dropped into Spain would be given away by the lack of **garlic** on their breath. To make 'the smelly substance' more pleasant to eat, he added it to chocolate bars. Lovely.

◄ '**Face cream**' was the codename for a strong chemical that fogged glass, useful for sabotaging optical instruments and creating indelible anti-German graffiti on windows and windscreens.

It could be made to look and smell like face cream, sun lotion or toothpaste. Unfortunately one batch of 'toothpaste' went out without instructions and was issued to agents with disastrous results.

► **Itching powder** was liberally sprinkled over uniforms for sailors and U-boat crews. The catalogue notes 'The greatest effect is produced by applying to the inside of underclothing'. At least one submarine was forced to return to base because the crew thought they'd caught a skin disease. The Norwegian Resistance took things a step further by powdering the inside of condoms being sent to the occupying German troops.

◄ Some SOE sabotage experts were insurance loss adjusters, who knew all about arson and fouling up machines. They may have suggested using this **abrasive powder** on train axles to cause unscheduled stops. Its effectiveness, however, was questionable. They should have just put leaves on the line.

126

◀ 'A short length, **silent murder weapon**' in the plain words of the SOE catalogue. The gun lived up your sleeve and could be easily shaken into your hand for use. Just don't forget it's there.

▼ These **Balinese wood carvings** were actually made of solid high explosive. The idea was that they'd be sold by agents posing as quayside hawkers to Japanese soldiers about to embark.

▲ An **explosive mule dropping** for blowing up car tyres in Italy. Other kinds of detonating dung were available: horse for other parts of Europe and camel for North Africa. The real thing was supplied to SOE by London Zoo and copied in plastic.

◀ Smoking these is definitely bad for your health. These **cigarettes** contain a pellet specifically designed to start fires. You lit the pellet end for an instant conflagration, the other for a delayed action. SOE also developed a cigarette that could fire a bullet.

Animals

FROM PARADOGS TO
WARRIOR BIRDS

PAGE 128
'Hello, Sailor!' **Venus**, the mascot of the destroyer HMS *Vansittart*, gives the bulldog spirit a sassy spin in this photograph from 1941.

PAGE 129
The **Dickin Medal** is the animals' Victoria Cross. One of the first was awarded to Judy, a Royal Navy mascot dog, for numerous life-saving feats in the Far East, including finding a spring on a desert island and saving four men from drowning. As if that wasn't enough, she was the only dog to be officially recognised as a POW, such was her importance to the morale of the soldiers held in a Japanese camp in Sumatra. The BBC broadcast her barks to a grateful nation in 1946.

IN 1943 THE PEOPLE'S Dispensary for Sick Animals (PDSA) founded the Dickin Medal to recognise acts of gallantry by animals. On the back of the medal are the words 'They also serve'. It's true: animals did serve in the Second World War, and in a remarkable variety of ways.

A surprisingly broad range of animals went into battle as military mascots – from mice to monkeys. Mascots offered companionship and entertainment to troops during stressful times and helped to foster *esprit de corps*. In return they could be pampered with special kennels or hammocks, and some were even given their own rank. The navy were such avid collectors of exotic animals that they had a special zoo set up back home.

Some animals helped in more direct ways, whether guard dogs, messenger bees or even the remarkable ammunition-carrying bear of the Polish Army. In the Far East elephants were used to manoeuvre planes on the ground; in Europe circus elephants were occasionally used to plough fields; in Berlin they helped to tidy up rubble after bombing raids.

As in the First World War, the humble pigeon was the most important animal participant – the UK alone used around 250,000. The birds were used to send messages from stranded troops, downed planes and secret agents. One of the most bizarre weapons races of the war was when Germany and Britain set up 'hawk squadrons' to attack each others' birds. Pigeons were the first and most numerous winners of Dickin Medals, receiving 32 of the 54 awarded during the war. They are celebrated today in museums (stuffed), with plaques, and even with their own memorial bird bath.

A **Persian kitten**
takes some time
out from learning
to hunt rats in a
specially made
hammock — or
should that be
cat's cradle? —
on the sloop HMS
Godavari, 1943.

Three receipts to
Tinker from Birmingham
for sale of her kittens to
the **Red Cross Penny-
a-Week Fund**, which
helped provide food
parcels to prisoners of
war and soldiers serving
abroad. Usually, people
contributed a penny from
their wage packet, but
Tinker was too paw (sorry).

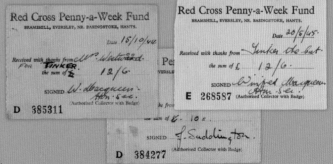

◀ The **ornate kennel** of Bully the squadron mascot, part of 'Grosvenor House' — a snug residence (with all modern conveniences) built by RAF airmen at their station in France, 1939.

'Acting Dog Pilot' Sammy signs an entry in his flying log book. Sammy was the dog of Flight Lieutenant Oliver Philpott, who took part in the Wooden Horse escape from a German POW camp in 1943 (see the Great Escapes chapter). He accompanied his master on non-operational flights.

Just Nuisance is the only dog to be officially enlisted in the Royal Navy, despite never making it further than the gangplank, where he liked to sleep (hence his nickname). A favourite of the sailors at the Simon's Town naval base in South Africa, the Great Dane became a formidable wartime morale booster and fundraiser. He is commemorated there with a statue and an annual lookalike competition.

Worried that Germany might bomb Britain with gas, some people took special precautions for their beloved pets. This **gas mask** was made for Roy, a sheepdog owned by the 5th Marchioness of Exeter. Military dogs were sometimes equipped with gas masks too. Bizarrely, the British even attempted to create masks for their sniffer dogs. It didn't work out.

So this is where they keep the shells? **Able Tortoise Snooks** takes his supper under the guns of HMS *Suffolk* in the Bay of Bengal, 1944. Snooks was definitely one of the more manageable naval mascots.

Barbara the polar bear greets her old shipmates at the unique 'sailors' zoo' on Whale Island near Portsmouth. The zoo housed an incredible collection of animals brought home by sailors, also including lions, kangaroos, emus — and of course a huge number of parrots.

When it came to superstitions, Churchill didn't monkey about. Legend had it that if the famous **apes** ever left the Rock of Gibraltar it would cease to be a British colony. So he ensured that their numbers were kept topped up. Here, the latest arrival is being checked in. Churchill took the same care with the ravens at the Tower of London.

◄ A plaque celebrating the largest — and hairiest — member of the Polish Army, **Corporal Wojtek**. This 8ft, 35 stone brown bear was adopted as a cub by the 22nd Artillery Supply Company. In addition to impressing the troops with his wrestling skills, he bravely delivered vital ammunition boxes — supposedly walking on his hind legs, as shown — throughout the fierce Battle of Monte Cassino in Italy. He retired to Edinburgh Zoo, where despite having picked up the typical soldiers' bad habits of drinking beer and smoking (well, mostly eating) cigarettes, he lived to the respectable age of 21.

Two **circus elephants**, Kiri and Many, clear wrecked vehicles from a street in Hamburg.

During the war both elephants had been used by the civil authorities in the city to clear wreckage after air raids and they continued in this role in the immediate aftermath of the war.

Eustace the piebald mouse was the mascot of the crew of a D-Day landing craft in 1944.

Despite many narrow squeaks, he returned safely to Britain, perhaps disappointed to find that cheese was even more heavily rationed in France.

◀ Salvo the fox terrier **'paradog'**. Dogs accompanied D-Day troops dropped behind German lines, sniffing out mines, traps and troops. They were given two months' intensive training, including how to angle themselves in the air — 'forepaws up and rear legs down'. But understandably on the day some of the dogs had to be encouraged out of the plane with the aid of a two-pound piece of meat.

▲ The **pigeon GI Joe** is attended by some slightly bemused officers and dignitaries at a medal ceremony at the Tower of London. The bird is credited with the 'most outstanding flight made by a United States Army homing pigeon in World War Two', travelling 20 miles in as many minutes to save British troops from being accidentally bombed by the Americans in Italy. Like many medal-winning pigeons he ended up stuffed and displayed in a museum, a fate that highly decorated soldiers are spared.

British beekeepers did their bit by donating honey to submarine crews. In China **bees** took a more front-line role, getting tiny messages through the Japanese lines. And in Ethiopia they were used as a weapon against the Italians. In the ultimate sting operation, the invaders' tanks were bombarded with beehives, causing several of them to swerve down a hillside and be destroyed.

THE COLORADO BEETLE.

GREATLY ENLARGED.

A DANGEROUS FOREIGN POTATO PEST.

WATCH YOUR POTATO PLANTS.

If you find Striped Beetles about ½ inch long, or red Grubs, eating the Potato Foliage, send specimens to the Ministry of Agriculture Laboratory, Milton Road, Harpenden, Herts.

As it says, 'There is a Maiden Form for every type of figure'— even the pigeon-chested. In 1944 the US government asked the brassiere company to make 28,500 special **vests** to protect carrier pigeons strapped to the chests of paratroopers dropped behind enemy lines. British paratroopers simply cut the end off an old sock and stuffed the bird in ...

In 1942 Germany planned to destroy the British potato crop by dropping 40 million spud-munching **Colorado beetles**. As a test, 40,000 were released over fields in Germany, but despite each one being painted brightly, only 100 could be found. So another 14,000 were dropped. This time just 57 were located. Having successfully conducted beetle warfare against themselves, the Germans shelved the plans.

Concerned that German agents in Britain were communicating using carrier pigeons, MI5 set up the **Special Falconry Unit**. Three peregrine falcons patrolled the coast and downed a total of 23 'pigeon agents'.

Unfortunately, all of them turned out to be British. On a happier note, two German pigeons were blown across the Channel and became 'prisoners of war'. A government memo records them 'working hard breeding English pigeons'.

British pigeons are commemorated in a park in the seaside town of Worthing with a monument dedicated to the **'Warrior Birds'** of the Second World War. It was designed to double as a bird bath 'for the pleasure and use of living birds'. In recent times, a special memorial service has been held there on 21 November of each year.

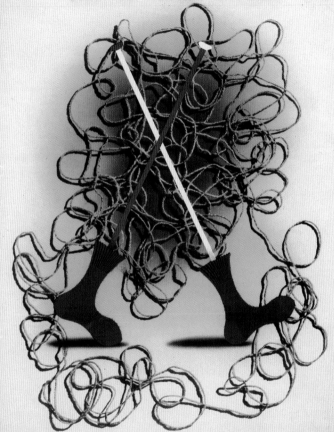

Home Fronts

FROM LUMINOUS FLOWERS
TO DOG WOOL

PAGE 140
British soldiers were issued with a measly four pairs of socks, so women back home were encouraged to get **knitting**. With peace in 1945 the government decided even fewer socks were needed and asked for one pair back from every soldier. The troops returned 1.5 million pairs. Let's hope they washed them first.

PAGE 141
A **luminous flower brooch**. A must-have for the stylish lady who wants to avoid collisions in the blackout. Less high-tech approaches to being seen in the dark included sewing white patches on to your clothes and leaving your shirt tails hanging out.

THE BLACKOUT WAS one of the first ways that the war affected Britain. It came into effect two days before the conflict was declared and a year before the Blitz started. Plunging the nation into darkness every night to avoid guiding enemy bombers took its toll. In 1939 the king's surgeon wrote that blackout accidents enabled the Luftwaffe 'to kill 600 British citizens a month without ever taking to the air'. The battle to be seen in the dark prompted solutions from wearing white clothing to carrying a luminous walking stick or even a white Pekinese.

Then there was rationing — not just of food but fuel, clothes and furniture. Britons had to cut back and, in the words of the campaign, 'Make Do and Mend'. Need a new skirt? Make one from an old pair of trousers. Holes in your clothes? Make war on moths. Don't have stockings? Try gravy browning. Recycling was practised, too, on a scale that we would envy today. Kitchen waste didn't just make compost — it could help to make planes and ammunition.

On both sides of the Atlantic and across the Empire there was a torrent of knitting for the troops. If you had a dog you could even combine knitting and recycling by using its 'wool' (although the Women's Institute admitted the results were generally inferior to sheep's wool).

But many women on the home front had heavier work to do. As men were called up, women stepped into roles in factories, heavy industry and agriculture. With minor adjustments to protective garb — no one had ever thought of a safety bra before — they proved remarkably good.

▲ Members of the Canine Defence League show off 'long sea boot stockings' they have knitted from the hair of their pet Samoyed. Other breeds that were deemed good for **'dog wool'** included Old English Sheepdog, Pekinese, Poodle, Chow, Golden Retriever, Cocker Spaniel, Pom and St Bernard.

◄ **Bones** were used to make glue for aircraft construction and to provide chemicals for ammunition. For a while the Ministry of Aircraft Production experimented with another equally unusual material in making planes – nettles. Paper made from nettle fibre could be nearly as strong as steel in certain circumstances.

A light (or rather dark) **bulb** from Brighton station. The fear was that even the tiniest light could guide enemy bombers. People met the challenge with all sorts of useful — and bizarre — innovations.

With windows covered, streetlights dimmed and car lights reduced to thin slits, getting around town in the blackout became a risky business. For anyone worried about blindly walking into the road, the answer was to attach this convenient **kerbfinder** to the end of a walking stick or umbrella.

▶ No, it's not a cunning zebra disguise to confuse invaders. Even in the countryside the blackout held hazards, and some farmers took to **painting their cows** to prevent car accidents.

Boredom was another unhappy consequence of the blackout. But not if you had '**Blackout – The Topical Game for Up to Five Players**', a dominos-like card game.

The popular *Brighter Blackout Book* also provided some light-hearted relief. It was designed to be easily read by torchlight, and included war-themed parlour games such as making a two-minute speech about 'How I like my egg' in the style of Mussolini.

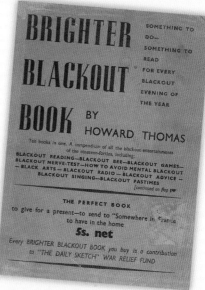

Some of the 150 members of the **Fiji Military Forces Knitting Circle**, who got together to knit socks for troops overseas. The champion sock knitters of the war, though, were the women of Australia, who made over 3 million pairs.

WEIRD WAR FACT

Britons were banned from sending knitting patterns abroad in case they contained coded messages to the enemy. It sounds dotty, but the censors had a point. The Belgian Resistance recruited little old ladies whose windows happened to overlook railway yards. As they knitted, they would drop a stitch for a troop train, purl one for an artillery train and so on, providing useful intelligence.
And in the run-up to D-Day, there was a British agent who travelled along the coast of France recording the German defences in knitting patterns.

Ready for action! It wasn't only socks that civilians sent to the troops.

Companies produced patterns for all sorts of knitted comforts, including jumpers, gloves, scarves and of course incredibly chic **headgear**. Hopefully the 'balaclava helmet with cape pieces' will come back into fashion soon.

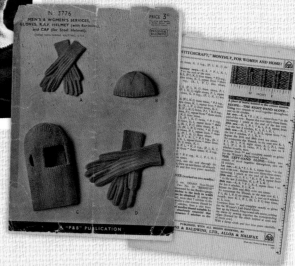

It wasn't just knitting and jam making. A few panels from an epic **embroidery** recording the many roles that women played in the war – everything from secret agents to lumberjacks (or 'lumberjills' as they were known). It was created by over 400 members of the Women's Institute and took four years to complete. It contains more than 2 million stitches.

Women were vital for agriculture too. The 120,000 strong **Women's Land Army** helped with everything from bringing in the harvest to catching rats.

These three are practising milking with artificial udders before being let loose on real ones. The cows were probably very grateful.

Let's hope she spat in his sandwich... As this spectacularly sexist **poster** attests, women in America and Britain also kept the wheels of heavy industry turning after men were called up to fight, with jobs including riveting, welding and repairing engines.

▲ That's not the best way to reduce accidents ... American factory workers unveil a new safety outfit for women, including the reassuringly robust, all-plastic **SAF-T-BRA**.

▶ Worried about the risks of women with long hair operating machinery, the **Royal Society for the Prevention of Accidents** issued this poster, one of series called 'Perverted Proverbs'. In America, the government asked film star Veronica Lake to change her hairstyle for the same reason. Her trademark 'peekaboo' style, of long locks covering half her face, was copied by factory workers with disastrous results.

PERVERTED PROVERBS

One good "perm" deserves a cover —

WEAR YOUR CAP

This unpleasant-looking character is called the **Squander Bug**. His job was to urge the public to save their money and invest it in war bonds. The American children's author Dr Seuss created his own version of the Squander Bug for use in war savings campaigns in the United States.

Plane talk from the Ministry of Labour. As well as frightening workers who are slapdash about **safety**, there's the reassuring notion that German planes are in fact held together with nails, string and glue. After the war, the artist, Philip Mendoza, became famous for cute anthropomorphic paintings of mice.

And he'll probably change the radio station without asking. After America entered the war, supplies of gasoline and natural rubber were rationed and car production was halted. The government encouraged **car sharing** and introduced a nationwide 35 mph speed limit, dubbed 'the victory speed'.

A flying pan. Shortages of aluminium for planes led to a government campaign encouraging people to donate pots and pans – **'Pans for Planes'**. Here, the process has gone into reverse: this pan is made from aluminium salvaged and recycled from the remains of crashed German aircraft.

Say it with celery. With production restricted to only essential items, glass factories carried on producing **flower vases** but labelled them to hold more useful items like celery.

To **save fuel**, the British population was encouraged to run only 5 inches of hot water in a bath. Many complied, including King George VI, who ordered the baths in Buckingham Palace to be marked in this way. Then he moved to Windsor Castle (just joking).

As clothes rationing was introduced, the government launched its **'Make Do and Mend'** campaign. People were urged do everything they could to extend the life of their clothes, from patching and darning to dealing with 'the moth menace'.

make war on moths

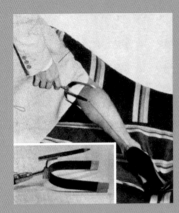

With silk and nylon being used for parachutes and other essential war items, women were forced to adapt, painting on fake stockings with make-up – or, at a pinch, gravy powder. The **fake seam** was the icing on the cake. Tricky to do though, unless you've got this contraption made of a screwdriver handle, a bicycle clip and an eyebrow pencil. In America the return of nylon stockings in 1945 prompted queues up to a mile long and several 'riots'.

In Britain **high heels** were condemned by the government's timber controller, Major Harris. 'Some of these heels are 3½ inches high,' he fumed, claiming that compulsory low heels would save Britain 50,000 tonnes of wood annually. At least one person pointed out that this figure looked dodgy. Was Britain really making over 400 million pairs of high heels a year?

With almost no other sources of silk, parachutes were a prize item. Here a British parachute has been turned into a **silk wedding dress**. In 1941 a German airman who bailed out over a small hamlet in the Midlands had his parachute seized by a group of women wielding pitchforks, brooms and scissors. It is said to have provided enough silk to make bloomers for all of them.

BETTER POT-LUCK

with
Churchill
today

THAN HUMBLE PIE

under
Hitler
tomorrow

DON'T WASTE FOOD!

Food and Drink

FROM CARROT LOLLIES TO
SQUIRREL TAIL SOUP

PAGE 156
If there's one thing that's guaranteed to get the British public's blood up it's a so-called 'pie' that's really just a casserole with a pastry lid. Trust Adolf Hitler to be one of those. At least you know where you are with Churchill's hearty pot of **leftovers.**

PAGE 157
What a cracking idea. **Fresh eggs** were rationed in 1942, so friends and relatives in the countryside posted what they could in special boxes. The alternative was the dreaded powdered egg from the US, which spawned some terrible recipes. Anyone for 'English Monkey' (scrambled powdered egg with cheese)? Just add tomatoes for mouthwatering 'Pink Monkey'!

IN 1939 BRITAIN IMPORTED roughly 70 per cent of its food. The government knew that Germany would try to starve the country by targeting shipping so it tasked the Ministry of Food with administering the rationing of many foodstuffs. Strict as this was, Britain was lucky to avoid the privations of many other nations, and the health of the population actually increased. Of course, faced with as little as one fresh egg or 50g of cheese a week, people didn't always feel lucky.

One way to try to keep things interesting was to substitute rationed ingredients. Some 'mock' dishes were fairly sensible, like using mutton for turkey (by Christmas 1943 only one in ten households in Britain could have the traditional bird). Some were utterly left field. Try making bananas from mashed parsnips and vanilla essence, or drinking potato beer, we dare you.

Campaigns were launched to promote abundant foods like carrots and spuds. Vegetables appeared in poster campaigns, cartoons and movies – even Disney came knocking. People were encouraged to grow their own food, too, and the 'Dig for Victory' campaign had a huge effect in raising public morale.

America's Spam was another great success story of the war, although its effect on morale was more mixed. At one point 15 million cans a week were being shipped overseas. There was no escape. Even if you went to a fancy restaurant, you might be served Escalope of Spam.

Of course you could always go totally 'off ration' by turning to nature. You could find gourmet grass recipes from a retired solicitor, and advice on stewing starlings and frying frogs from a French nobleman. Suddenly Spam didn't seem so bad after all.

A silent cinema-style **melodrama promoting potatoes,** an abundant crop.

Driven mad by another meal of cold sausage and pickles, a father rages out of the house. He returns to find his wife and daughter have prepared a delicious dish of potatoes. He begs forgiveness and his wife promises (or perhaps threatens) him, 'There are 199 other ways of cooking them.'

"Emmaline, can you ever forgive me? These potatoes are delicious!"

EAT MORE SPUDS

MOCKERY COOKERY

A few wartime workarounds for scarce ingredients

Mock apple pie
Replace the apples with ... 50 Ritz crackers (this recipe was invented by the manufacturer of Ritz crackers, by the way)

Mock apricot flan
Replace the apricots with ... carrots

Mock goose
Replace the goose with ... lentils

Mock turkey
Replace the turkey with ... lamb

Mock banana
Replace the banana with ... parsnips and vanilla essence

Actor Derrick De Marney auctions a very small **banana** at a fair in London, 1943. The fruit was virtually unseen in Britain after 1940 and this one fetched £5, the equivalent of over £200 today.

You can have your cake, but you can't eat it. These wartime **wedding cake covers** were made of paper and plaster and sat over the real cake, which was a great deal smaller and dowdier owing to rationing. The covers were passed from one wedding to the next.

DOCTOR CARROT the Children's best friend

VIT-A

◀ If your child's best friend is a giant talking carrot, seek help. Early in the war there was a surplus of **carrots** and the government encouraged the public to eat them in place of rationed foods. One ruse was to claim that the vitamin A in carrots aided night vision. The public eagerly tucked in, hoping they'd be able to see better in the blackout. Walt Disney even got in on the act, offering the government the characters 'Pop Carrot' and his kids 'Carroty George' and 'Clara Carrot'.

▶ The **carrot ice lolly** from 1941. Presumably inspired by sugar rationing, this is proof that the carrot is definitely not the child's best friend. The lolly may have been washed down with 'carrolade', a lemonade substitute made from carrot and swede juice.

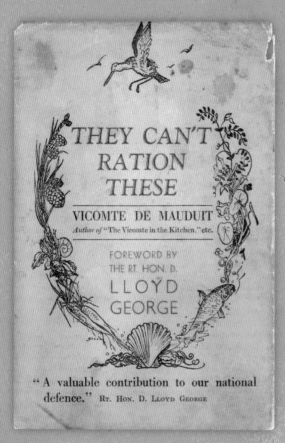

French gourmet chef Georges, Vicomte de Mauduit solved the problem of rationing by turning to 'nature's larder'. His book *They Can't Ration These* includes recipes for such unusual delicacies as dandelion fritters, squirrel tail soup, hedgehog stew and roast sparrows on toast.

No, it's not a campaign to promote eating zoo animals. This **1939 exhibition** at London Zoo informed the public about growing their own crops (more carrots ...) and keeping livestock. The animals at the zoo suffered rationing too. Fish in particular was very expensive, and the poor pelicans had to make do with meat covered in cod liver oil.

'Charles Wyse-Gardner' was the pen name of Major L H Chase, who pioneered the use of barn-shaped cloches (glass covers) to **extend the vegetable growing season**. He also wrote the memorably titled *Baccy – Grow and Smoke Your Own.*

A patriotic dress covered in **'Dig for Victory'** slogans and pictures of turnips, radishes, carrots, spinach, celery and beet. The Dig for Victory campaign encouraged civilians to supplement their diet with homegrown vegetables. It proved a hit and the number of allotments increased from 815,000 in 1939 to 1.4 million in 1943.

Even Beefeaters need vegetables.

Here the Yeoman Warders are growing their own in the dry moat of the **Tower of London**. This was just one of many unlikely locations converted to allotments as part of the Dig for Victory campaign, along with parks and even sports pitches.

Mrs Prendergast of Balham refuses to let her **air-raid shelter** get in the way of growing vegetables.

She has simply replanted the plants on top of the shelter, and now has crop of lettuce, beetroots and marrows on the way.

Mr Branson, a retired solicitor from Clapham, collects **grass** clippings for dinner.

He believed that grass made 'a most delightful meal' and campaigned for Britons to make it a key part of their diet, with pamphlets including *Recipes for Grass* and *Grass for All*. Later in the war he gave lectures to commandos on living off the land.

STOP PUFFIN AND BLOWING!

TEA REVIVES YOU

As the famous song from the 1930s says, 'Everything stops for tea.' Factory bosses wanted to make sure that it didn't stop for too long though, as this **poster** shows. In fact, a study of factory workers suggested that the real problem was mid-afternoon 'lavatory-mongering' (a lengthy chat in the toilets).

Merely to remind you that . . . .

TIME FLIES

(and especially where urgent repair jobs are concerned)

It's a well-known fact that the British run on **tea**. So, when war was declared, the government wasn't taking any chances. Within two days it took control of all tea and ordered that the huge reserves kept in London should be spread around the country to protect them from bombing.

A **Spitfire pilot** refuels with tea and a sandwich in 1944.

Although the tea ration for civilians only stretched to a few weak cups a day, the government made sure there was more for those in the armed forces and those in vital and demanding roles on the home front, such as firemen and miners.

Tea wasn't just important for morale in Britain. In 1941 British bombers dropped at least **75,000 bags of tea** over Dutch cities. This 'tea from heaven' carried the Netherlands Flag and the words, 'The Netherlands will rise again. Greetings from the Free Netherlands East Indies. Chins up.'

◄ Surely the most popular posting in the navy? In 1945 HMS *Menestheus* was converted into a **floating brewery** to supply soldiers in the Pacific with beer.
At the same time, the US military created a floating ice cream parlour that could produce ten gallons of ice cream every seven seconds.

▶ Apparently the Welsh labourer shown here stated, 'It may be dear, it may be thin, but there ain't no bad beer.' He might have felt differently if he'd been drinking one of the experimental **wartime potato beers**. At best they tasted, well, 'potatoey'. At worst they caused spectacular attacks of wind.

The long-range fuel tank of a Spitfire being filled with beer.

The 'joy juice' was donated by a brewery and flown to Allied troops in Normandy after D-Day, getting nicely chilled in the process. The **beer runs** stopped after Customs & Excise complained that the relevant export tax wasn't being paid. Spoilsports.

Right on the beam...
PLANKED **SPAM***

PLANKED **SPAM***

Score a whole Spam and rub with brown sugar. Surround it on the plank with tomato slices capped with large mushrooms doused in butter. Bake 25 minutes in hot oven, then ring with mashed potatoes and slip back in the oven for quick browning. Bring it to table, plank and all....and be greeted with cheers.

COLD OR HOT **SPAM** HITS THE SPOT!

HORMEL GOOD FOODS

*"Spam" is a registered trademark. It identifies a meat product—packed only in 12-ounce tins—made exclusively by Geo. A. Hormel & Co., Austin, Minn.

▶ This Royal Navy **sausage-making** crew averaged 18,000 sausages a day. Wartime sausages were nicknamed 'bangers' for a reason. Precious meat was heavily padded out with fat and water, which meant the sausages sizzled aggressively when cooked and were liable to fill with steam and explode. In 2016 a scientist concluded that today's more meaty sausages are around half as loud in the pan as their wartime counterparts.

US Army Food Slang

Army chicken – franks and beans
Army strawberries – prunes
Axle grease – butter
Bags of mystery – sausages
Bottled sunshine – beer
Dog food – corned beef hash
Ham that didn't pass its physical – Spam
Moo juice – milk
Pep tire – doughnut
Sea dust – salt
Spuds with the bark on – unpeeled potatoes
Tiger meat – beef

Does eating the plank as well make the **Spam** tastier? The war gave Spam a bit of a bad reputation. Tins of the American 'miracle meat' were shipped to troops and civilians around the world in incredible quantities. Familiarity bred contempt, particularly with the heaviest consumers: American soldiers. The inventor of Spam had a bulging 'scurrilous file' of hate mail from GIs.

Time Out

FROM BALLET DOGFIGHTS TO SMOKING DUMMIES

PAGE 172
Sailors and children play **pass the matchbox** on the deck of HMS *Sapphire*. The officers and men gave a tea party to 40 children from a village near their base in Harwich. The men went without their chocolate ration for weeks before so that the children could have a plentiful supply.

PAGE 173
You wouldn't call Gunner Jimmy Turner a **dummy** to his face. He was nearly 5ft tall and could speak, smoke and spit just like a real soldier. He could even be operated remotely from the side of the stage by his ventriloquist partner, Sergeant Walter Huntley. They performed together to civilians and soldiers across Britain as part of the army's 'Stars in Battledress' unit.

EVEN DURING A WAR — perhaps even more so — people need to be entertained and find ways to escape from the hardships of life.

Obviously it was tricky to do that on the front line. Where possible, games and sports were organised, as were concerts and theatricals by professional entertainers and enthusiastic troops. The navy had particular challenges, which it met with everything from raft races to fancy-dress board games. Sailors were particularly keen on theatricals at Christmas, a time when any distraction was welcome on ships far from home.

Keeping entertained was a challenge on the home front, too. British workers were encouraged to 'Holiday at Home' and 'Stay Put This Summer' to increase efficiency and keep the railways clear for war work. Television had stopped, for the few that had sets. Toys became plainer — even teddy bears slimmed down to save on stuffing. Things got so bad that trainspotting took off as a hobby.

Of course there were films and radio, and the government laid on concerts, dances, fêtes and other entertainments. Workers could get involved in lunchtime ballet or revues as well. After initially being suspended, professional sports resumed on a smaller scale. The football league was reorganised regionally to reduce travelling.

For POWs in the larger camps the daily routine was designed to provide ways of beating boredom — and to stop them thinking about digging tunnels, no doubt. Prisoners could borrow books from camp libraries and attend university classes. They formed choirs and orchestras. They held sports competitions and staged plays with remarkable professionalism — and outrageously fabulous outfits.

War artists: British **soldiers learn to paint** in an army college in the grounds of the Palazzo Pitti in Florence, 1945. This painting is by artist Carel Weight, whose other wartime works included a dramatic four-panel piece, *Escape of the Zebra from the Zoo during an Air Raid*, based on a real event in London in 1941.

▲ Two days before Britain entered the war, the BBC pulled the plug on England's **television** service. There were fears that bombers could lock on to its signal, which was the strongest in Europe. The last programme was a Mickey Mouse cartoon. Sadly viewers missed *Practical Household Suggestions* and *Interest Film: West of Inverness* later that day. In 1945, the same cartoon was played as the first programme. Typical, another repeat.

▶ Without television, people were forced to make their own entertainment. Here, a member of the Red Cross supervises as a young boy plays '**Drive a nail into Hitler's coffin**' at a fête in central London. The aim was to get the nail in within three swipes, although young children were given a head start.

It's 1940 and Europe is going to pieces.

Try putting it back together with this **jigsaw puzzle** from New Zealand, complete with swastika-shaped tiles. When assembled, the jigsaw shows a map of Europe with its borders as they were in summer 1940 before the fall of France.

Women workers at a Hurricane factory prepare to stage a **ballet dog fight** in the canteen for the rest of the staff. The main characters are dressed as bird-like aircraft. The Ballet Rambert and the Old Vic theatre company also organised tours to factories and other local venues.

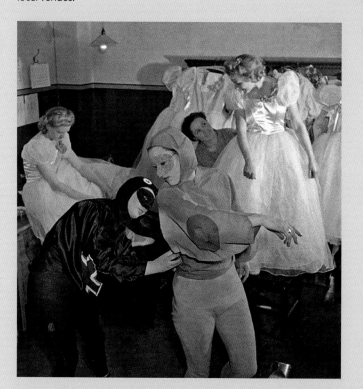

As the war approached, **Meccano** aeroplane kits were modified so they wouldn't be useful to the Germans for training pilots and gunners. Production ceased altogether after the war started, but the beloved toy still had a role to play. Sets were used to rehabilitate injured soldiers and to entertain bored POWs. The government even used Meccano for testing potential engineering officers for the Royal Engineers.

To keep the railways clear for moving troops and freight and to maximise productivity, the government encouraged workers to **holiday at home**. Local authorities did their best to bring the seaside to town with concerts and games in parks, but the Ministry of Labour bemoaned: 'It is really rather a hopeless task to convert Wolverhampton into Weston Super Mare and Bolton into Blackpool.'

Peggy Franks and her friend Pinkie Barnes have taken the 'holiday at home' message to heart and are enjoying **tea in the sunshine** in the garden. A medicine ball is next to them, a rather hefty substitute for a beach ball.

▲ Seamen play officers at **'Grand Uckers'**, a kind of fancy dress Ludo popular in the navy. The rules? Decide what to do about a 'bum throw' and 'cocky die' then get your counters down the pipes and round the board and back home. Remember that a 'mixi-blob' has no blocking powers, unlike a 'blob'. Clear?

▶ The crew of HMS *Kelvin* preparing for a **raft race** in the harbour at Malta. Some of the men are in small Maltese fishing boats whilst others are in dinghies probably taken from the ship. When ships were in port, organised sports offered sailors clean and healthy fun — unlike the port itself.

▼ A **snowman** on the quarterdeck of the destroyer HMS *Kelvin* made by the officers and some of the crew, complete with helmet and gas mask. Nuts and bolts are used for the eyes, nose and mouth, and a metal plate for a beard.

▶ Sometimes one **pet monkey** is not enough. First Lieutenant John Harmer is joined by his pals for Christmas dinner on HMS *Westminster* in 1941. Having two monkeys was not the end of this officer's eccentricities. Legend has it his party trick was to leap onto a table and eat a wine glass.

▼ A very dry dock. Members of a German U-boat crew captured in the Mediterranean sculpt a **submarine out of sand** at Agami camp near Alexandria in Egypt in 1941.

A seaman hauls a **Christmas tree** to the masthead of HMS *Turquoise* in accordance with custom. Other naval Christmas traditions included having the commanding officer and the youngest sailor swap places for the day, and the officers serve the Christmas dinner to the men.

Meanwhile, at an airbase near London members of the US 44th Bombardment Group ('The Flying Eightballs') hoist a **bicycle up a telegraph pole**. It was probably just for a laugh rather than to honour any particular custom.

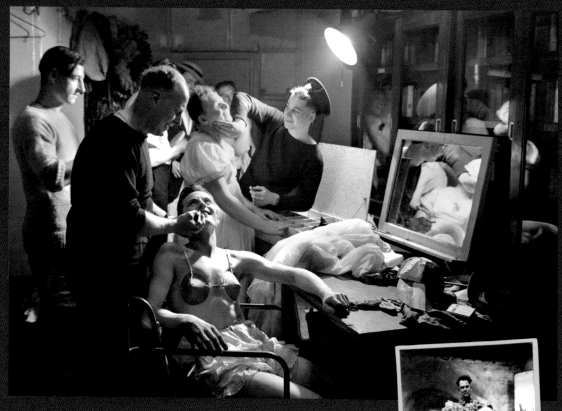

▲ A couple of stokers put on their war paint as they prepare for a **Christmas concert** on board HMS *Tyne* at Scapa Flow. The absence of women on board usually required some of the men to dress up.

▶ A photograph from a production at the POW theatre, Ofladium, set up at Stalag 383 in southern Germany. Extensive research has failed to uncover who is wearing this **costume** and why. We can assume it was either a theatrical revue or a particularly inventive escape attempt.

▼ **British POWs dress up** with varying success for a show at Stalag Luft III camp. At Colditz camp, a French officer put his act to the ultimate test by trying to escape dressed as a woman. He was only rumbled when he dropped his watch and a fellow prisoner gallantly asked the sentries to return it to him.

▶ A **posse of cowboys** (and a couple of cowgals) from another production at Stalag 383. As well as producing impressive costumes POWs produced ornate programmes, each one created by hand using a production lineof artists, sign-writers and typists.

Denis Houghton played second flute in the Changi camp orchestra in Singapore. He made this **flute** from two stirrup pumps, two fire extinguishers, brass parts from 15-inch naval guns, bicycle spokes, a spring from a broken watch and a packet of sewing needles.

The impressive **inter-barrack darts trophy** from Bandoeng, a Japanese POW camp in Java. It was awarded by the camp newspaper, *Mark Time*, in 1943. The trophy was made by British POWs from wood, bamboo and aluminium from Dutch mess tins. It was designed by Sid Scales, who went on to be a celebrated newspaper cartoonist in New Zealand.

Lieutenants Andrew Biggar and Ronald Eastman built this **miniature loom** to pass the time in Oflag VIIB Eichstatt. They used it to weave a jumper and a tartan scarf. Later they built a larger loom, which a fellow POW used to make a fetching tweed skirt.

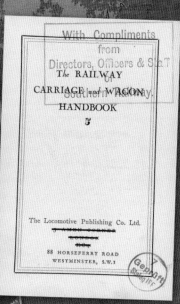

RAILWAY
CARRIAGE & WAGON
HANDBOOK

With Compliments
from
Directors, Officers & Staff
The RAILWAY
CARRIAGE *and* WAGON
HANDBOOK
3

The Locomotive Publishing Co. Ltd.

88 HORSEFERRY ROAD
WESTMINSTER, S.W.I

A book sent to Stalag IV-F by Southern Railway. Obviously the opportunities for **trainspotting** were limited in POW camps unless you escaped. Books about trains were required reading for boys before the war, and trainspotting was a hugely popular hobby. The first book of engine numbers was published in 1942 and sold out almost immediately.

WEIRD WAR FACT

In one POW camp in Bavaria three passionate birdwatchers installed 27 nesting boxes and recruited 30 men to watch them. Birdwatchers were ideal observers for escape attempts, as they could watch the guards without arousing suspicion.

They didn't always make ideal escapees, though. One, Peter Conder, insisted on dragging 17 notebooks of bird observations with him. Amazingly he made it, and after the war he became head of the Royal Society for the Protection of Birds (RSPB).

Celebrations

in Whitehall,
London on VE Day,
8 May 1945.

Picture List

All images © IWM unless otherwise stated. Every effort has been made to contact all copyright holders, the publishers will be glad to make good in future editions any error or omissions brought to their attention

PAGE 6-7
Introduction

H 2646A, AMY 684, D 15980, EA 31, D 18484

PAGE 8-25
Supreme Leaders

H 2626A, Art.IWM PST 18348, Art.IWM ART LD 7226, HU 90973, HU 5234, NYP 12886, HU 48102, HU 10180, HU 53442, LBY K 702311, H 25966, EPH 1406_A, ©Amanda Slater, this image is licensed under the terms of a Creative Commons Attribution-Share Alike 2.0 Generic license, EPH 9068 A, A 22451, E 15347, ©William Warby, this image is licensed under the terms of a Creative Commons Attribution 2.0 Generic license, TWM_FISH_170915_0005 ©www.thousandwordmedia.com, E 26640, HU 59832, LBY 29927_1, EPH 9470, Art.IWM PST 17009 (detail), LBY 81746 1, Library of Congress, EPH 9509, IWM FLM 1506, HU 10180

PAGE 26-41
Keep Calm

D 3948, LBY 18463_1, EQU 2597, Art.IWM PST 14814, D 2771, Documents 11929_J_1, D 15980, UNI 13456, HU 85532, HU 73594, HU 50154, FIR 3256, H 3640, LBY PROC 770_A, H 4731, EPH 10074, illustration by David Hopkins, by kind permission of Heritage Lincolnshire, LBY K. 73237, H 415

PAGE 42-59
Camouflage and Visual Deception

H 8059, Courtesy Dayle Tyrrell, Paige Auction, Art.IWM ART LD 3024, Boeing Aircraft Factory ©Tom Philo Photography, D 16491, Art.IWM ART LD 3019, H 3306, H 3307, H 3034, EPH 11145, EPH 11145_A, EPH 11145_B Courtesy of Craig & Rose Ltd., HU 86237, A 5433, A 23969, ADM 212-129, NYP 13306, Art.IWM ART LD 2759, Art.IWM PST 15897, Jasper Maskeleyne Variety Poster from the British Music Hall Society, E 18461, TR 180, H 42535, H 42531, B 8297, H 42530, LBY 33475_2

PAGE 60-75
Soldiering On

H 18619, Art.IWM PST 15913, HU 65958, A 16152, CH 2820, CH 11417, CH 2851, INS 7533, INS 7532, Sea Squatters Club Courtesy of Ens. Loyd Malcolm 'Mac' Bettis, INS 5332, INS 6573, INS 8111, INS 6658, INS 5306, INS 4126, INS 6603, Art.IWM PST 2850 Courtesy of Luis Rubio, LBY PROC 213, Art.IWM PST 2846, Art.IWM PST 2847, HU 65964, 4109.50.1, LBY K. 96/2863, LBY K. 92/242, ©Sean Hayford Oleary. This image is licensed under the terms of a Creative Commons Attribution-Share Alike 2.0 Generic license, TR 2891

PAGE 76-89
Great Escapes

HU 4226, HU 4225, Docs.13456 – 05/65/1A, HU 82265, HU 49533, EPH 637, EQU 4058, CH 1405, HU 21225, EPH 4528, HU 1612, EPH 9976, LBY K. 12/1336, EPH 3604, LBY 00/562, EPH 4530, EPH 1141, ©Johannes Niebler. This image is licensed under the Creative Commons Attribution-Share Alike 3.0 Unported license, EPH 2206, EPH 1729, EPH 10930, LBY 562_1

PAGE 90-101
Keep Mum

Art.IWM PST 13946, Art.IWM PST 17414, Art.IWM PST 14429, Art.IWM PST 16713, Art.IWM PST 16750, Art.IWM PST 16745, Art.IWM PST 16570, Art.IWM PST 16703, Art.IWM PST 13913, Art.IWM PST 13911, Art.IWM PST 13933, Art.IWM PST 13910, INF 3/271 Courtesy of the National Archives, AMY 137-1.44/1.54/3.48/4.40, INF3-227 Courtesy of the National Archives, D 20369

PAGE 102-115
Weapons and Inventions

Q 69051, FRE 7905, AMY 684, FIR 6243, © Jon Olav Eikenes, US Government Public Domain, A 29185, Popular Mechanics magazine, ©Estate of James Lewicki, MH 956, Art.IWM ART LD 5593, MOD 426, 4110.90.1, H 37859, MH 2214, H 41966, MAR 564, FLM 1627, T 54

PAGE 116-127
Secret Agents

EQU 12207, EPH 8310, Documents.16947, © National Portrait Gallery, National Archives, EPH 1282, PHO 225, EPH 10074, WEA 4147, FIR 3683, WEA 3040, Docs.16947, HU 61069, D 3744, EPH 10283, Documents.16947

PAGE 128-139
Animals

A 3998, EPH 9321, A 18814, Documents.701, C 102, Documents.13456, 'Just Nuisance' by Jean Doyle image ©Paul Mannix, EPH 2907, A 26465, HU 45273, GM 4456, Art.IWM ART LD 6502, A 24120, BU 11449, EA 31, HU 2899 Courtesy of PDSA, Maidenform Collection, Archives Center, National Museum of American History, Smithsonian Institution, TR 1951, Art.IWM PST 20608, ©Michael L. Baird, ©Daniela Gargiulo

PAGE 140-155
Home Fronts

Art.IWM PST 2978, EPH 9539, Art.IWM PST 14693, British Pathé, EPH 4583, EPH 9536, HU 36167, EPH 519, LBY 82/1706, K 7353, EPH 4229, Art.IWM ART LD 766, NARA 44-PA-911, NARA 86-WWT-33-41, Art.IWM PST 14483 & Art.IWM PST 14340 reproduced by kind permission of the Royal Society for Prevention of Accidents, Art.IWM PST 3406, NARA 516143, EPH 4627, EPH 2230, D 11080, Art.IWM PST 8297, Popular Mechanics magazine, UNI 1052, D 14826

PAGE 156-171
Food and Drink

Art.IWM PST 3108, EPH 1772, NMV 706A, D 14677, EPH 1062, Art.IWM PST 8105, British Pathé, Booksmith, Art.IWM PST 8106, LBY K. 81/3465, EPH 6395, HU 63758, HU 63827A, LBY K. 13/465, Leonard Joel Auction House, Art.IWM PST 3703, HU 87716, National Liberation Museum, A 9988, D 18484, CH 13488, Hormel Foods, A 1666

PAGE 172-189
Time Out

A 21101, EPH 10146, Art.IWM ART LD 5700, COM 645, D 14682, EPH 10815, D 11137, Art.IWM PST 4934, D 16038, A 196, A 4354, A 2770, A 6482, A 7104, A 21070, FRE 5483, A 13436, Docs.17465 ©Estate of R A Wheeler, HU 21146, EPH 801, EPH 182, EPH 5847, LBY 94/68, TR 2876

Acknowledgements

Many thanks to the staff of Imperial War Museums for their help, especially Caitlin Flynn, Madeleine James and Ian Carter. And thanks again to Phil Gilderdale and Carole Ash for their great design work.